INSPIRATION IN THE BIBLE

ABOUT THE BOOK

Karl Rahner, professor of dogmatic theology at Innsbruck, examines the question of scriptural inspiration with the conviction that the whole issue could benefit by being completely re-thought. He suggests, therefore, an entirely new approach to the mystery, in which the Scriptures are seen primarily as an essential and constitutive element of the Apostolic Church, and their inspiration simply as part of the activity of God in establishing the Church as the guardian of the deposit of faith. The study is intentionally provocative, but no one conversant with the subject of inspiration can fail to find here food for thought and reflection.

QUAESTIONES DISPUTATAE

KARL RAHNER

INSPIRATION IN THE BIBLE

HERDER

FREIBURG

———————

NELSON

EDINBURGH-LONDON

Original edition "Über die Schriftinspiration", Herder, Freiburg

Translated by Charles H. Henkey, Ph.D., S.T.D.

Nihil Obstat: Carolus Davis, S.T.L.
Censor deputatus

Imprimatur: E. Morrogh Bernard, Vic. Gen.
Westmonasterii, die 22a, Aprilis, 1961

Library of Congress Catalog Card Number: 61-10179

First published in West Germany © 1961 Herder KG

Made and printed in West Germany by Herder

CONTENTS

INTRODUCTION

THERE is no need to furnish a justification for dealing with our subject. Its importance is obvious within the realm of the Christian and Roman Catholic religion. When we say that Christianity is a "book-religion" we are stating something that is right and important, but if such a statement is taken in some exclusive sense it would be open to misunderstandings, and false.

Our subject concerns the student of dogma and the Biblical scholar. It deals with a point of defined doctrine, with the very essence of those books and writings which in daily use should serve, not only as directives for theological knowledge, but also as guides for Christian living during man's pilgrimage here on earth.

On the other hand, however, we could hardly maintain that theological interest among Roman Catholics is focused today on the problem of the inspiration of the Scriptures. To be honest, we must confess that, on the average, Roman Catholic Scripture scholars, although by no means denying or doubting the inspiration of the Bible, prefer not to touch it at all in their exegetical work. Perhaps they act as if it had little bearing on the performance of their tasks as exegetes. For them, inspiration signifies, in practice, the non-errancy of the Bible. This non-errancy is based upon inspiration, and constitutes, as it were, a negative norm for exegesis, but has no further meaning for the exegetes.

We may ask whether it is only the exegetes and the rationalist and historical atmosphere of their studies that are responsible for this state of affairs, or whether there is a real need for re-thinking the whole problem of inspiration.

Our study is not concerned with Biblical theology, but with dogma. That means that its starting point is not the Bible itself and whatever statements can be found therein concerning inspiration, but the teaching on inspiration as it is established in its basic traits by the magistracy of the Church and explained and expanded in scholastic theology. Such an approach, if not the only possible one, is certainly legitimate. Whether it is to be recommended in this particular case will have to be judged by its results.

As we are here trying to handle a subject of large dimensions in a short essay, some reservations must be made, even here at the beginning. It is permissible to consider that, in the realm of theology as in the realm of the sciences, it is legitimate to experiment, to work with hypotheses, remembering that, even in their originator's opinion, they may turn out to be barren when tested by the criticism of his colleagues and confrères working in sacred theology. Theology is certainly anything but a mummified structure of thought. It can create openings for adventures of the mind and of the heart, if we have but the courage to embark upon them, and both the courage and humility to retrace our steps as soon as we become aware of having erred. This qualification is made in all seriousness. If we are convinced that in theology, as elsewhere, there are real problems which still require better, clearer, more comprehensive and possibly even simpler solutions, we shall certainly not begrudge having to face such problems. Nor shall

7

we be likely to confuse brotherly criticism with official censorship if a proposed hypothesis is proved to be inadequate, or even false.

To ask questions about a doctrine which, in its basic dogmatic contents is beyond discussion, is not tantamount to doubting or contesting a doctrine of the Faith. It is the unavoidable business of the theologian who refuses to find comfortable support for his own mental laziness in the definitions of Denzinger. He who believes that, even in the most intimate circles, only final and absolute solutions ought to be discussed, shows his incapacity for seeing any new answer or problem in theology.

In this paper we plan first to expose some related problems concerning the traditional concept of inspiration; secondly, we shall submit the outline of a systematic structure which, in the third part, will have to prove itself as the answer to the problems raised in the first place.

The relationship between "old" and "new" in our case is the same as it generally is in theology: usually we tend to see only the things which have always been seen, which are known to all and which are not surprising. However, we will try to see the old truths and facts in a perspective in which certain correlations will become visible between these old truths, to which up to now little or no attention has been paid. They may help us to recognize the simple harmony of the whole, the basic principle of all details.

I

THE BASES OF THE PROBLEM

TO mention some of the problems on inspiration is not to list all of them, nor to maintain that those to be discussed here are the most important ones. We are concerned simply with those problems which, in our mind, give rise to the hypothesis proposed in the second part of the essay. This was the only reason for their selection.

We assume the acceptance of the traditional concept of inspiration, which is partly defined, partly laid down by the official teaching of the Church, and is partly the concept formed by the common opinion of scholastic theology. It is not our purpose to criticize this concept, nor to propose to change it. If we had any intentions in this regard, it would be only to show by raising some questions that this concept of inspiration, implicitly acceptable as it seems to us, has a certain formal abstractness. Easily overlooked as it is, this abstract concept is sometimes regarded as an adequate, material and factual description of the process of inspiration, though on closer examination we might prefer it to be more meaningful in the way we hope to propose.

We thus assume the traditional teaching of the Church as binding. The Scriptures have God as their author: he is the "author" in the literary sense of the word, because he inspired the Scriptures. This inspiration does not consist in the fact that the

9

Scriptures have been accepted as canonical by the Church,[1] nor that they interpret free from error the revelation of God.

It would be more true to say that inspiration consists in the fact that God supernaturally illuminates the human author in the perception of the content and of the essential plan of the book,

---

[1] This statement contains, of course, more problems than one might normally think. We might remember that, according to the teaching of the Church and to the testimony of the Bible, an inspired author may make use of "sources". How far is this use of sources permissible? How far, to use plain language, is he allowed to "plagiarize"? Can he use his sources in such a way that his "authorship" (meaning his own work minus the contributions of his sources to the inspired text) would consist of nothing in effect but the appropriation and approbation of sources? An author who only "copies" would, according to our present moral judgement, not be an author at all; for our normal concept of authorship includes the claim for originality. But should it be necessarily excluded through such copying – of which again the technical performance may vary – that the writer might nevertheless regard his work as the expression (indeed by transcription) of his thoughts and, consequently, as his own, admittedly not very original work? Is, for instance, the original author of a religious hymn, or of a psalm, necessarily inspired? Or could we maintain that the inspiration appertains to him who introduced this psalm into the official use of the synagogue, who has recognized the hymn as an authentic expression of his own and of the community's religious conviction, claiming it as his work, unoriginal though it may be? If this second question can be answered affirmatively, then an act of acceptance of writings by a competent person or persons as an, as it were, official pronouncement of the opinion of the community or of the Church, might constitute a sufficient reason on the one hand for adequate authorship and for inspiration. On the other hand, we shall be closer still to the phenomenon of approbation of writings through the Church. We must not, therefore, regard such authorship as simply identical with that later approbation, which the Church has rejected as constituting the essence of inspiration, or its vehicle. If, for instance, the Pope issues an encyclical letter, he is to be considered as its author, even when he thereby only approves of writings actually composed by his

and moves him to write freely all and only that which God wants to be written. Moreover, God stands by him in order that the mentally conceived and freely-willed work should also be properly performed. Here we can presuppose the validity and dogmatic sources of this concept.

We come now to the problems with which we are going to deal.

theologians as the expression of his own teaching function. He remains the author, even though he has not changed a single word in the text. Naturally, in such a case we might distinguish between literary and "authoritative" authorship. But the question remains, how to distinguish accurately between them and whether the latter kind of authorship is the real and genuine article. This may certainly be the case even though it differs from the former kind, which we usually imply when speaking of the "author" of any book. Consequently we may wonder whether this second type of authorship could not be sufficient for the essential purpose of inspiration. Ultimately everything may depend on the will and intention of him who gives the approval. He may approve it as the opinion of the original author, or as an expression of his own opinion. In the former case, he could not possibly be the bearer of inspiration, whereas in the latter case he could well be one. If, for example, St. Paul wrote, as is generally thought, the Epistle to the Hebrews, in which he approves of the theological work of one of his disciples, who then was it who was actually inspired? We shall have to say that it was St. Paul. For the Church recognizes the inspired character of this treatise as an epistle of St. Paul. But how can St. Paul, according to this view, arguable as it may be, still be the inspired author of the epistle to the Hebrews, unless he could become such through the simple approbation of a work, by approving it also as an expression of his own and not merely by declaring it to be in agreement with his own opinion? But if this is possible, we might regard it as useful at least to have a more exact formulation of the teaching on the non-identity of approbation by the Church and inspiration.

The German theologian Pesch has suggested in his *De inspiratione,* n. 412, that there is nothing against the idea that a man should be inspired to write something that, on a mere human level, has already been written

11

1. The Two Authors

God is the literary author of the Scriptures, he is their author. This is stated by the dogmas of the Council of Trent and of the Vatican Council, at least, if we understand in the light of tradition the expression, *Deum habent auctorem* (D 1787, cf. 783), and have regard to *Spiritu Sancto dictante* (D 783), and *Spiritu Sancto inspirante* (D 706), which occur in this context.[2] Now according to the general view of the theologians, it is not denied that the human originator of the Holy Scrip-

by someone else. The question of plagiarism can be ignored, because in this respect the situation always varies according to the kinds of literature and changing views in different times. We may, therefore, hold that authorship can imply the appropriation of someone else's writings. In this case God would become the author of this divine inspiration in causing this act of appropriation. God becomes the author through this act, not through causing the earlier original work to be written. It is thus conceivable that this human act of appropriation has been connected *a priori* with an intention to make this appropriated piece of writing a book of the holy community of the Church and it is actually this intention which brings about the appropriation.

All this is not mentioned here in order to propose a complete thesis already at the beginning of our discussion. The reason is really to show by some such groping "exercise" that there could exist a difference between the formal content (which alone is implied by the teaching authority) of some statements about inspiration, and their material content, given by us, as it were, without clear sanction either by the matter itself or by the teaching authority.

[2] On this matter see A. Bea, "Deus auctor Sacrae Scripturae. Herkunft und Bedeutung der Formel" in: *Angelicum,* 20 (1943), pp. 16–31. We would admit that, in our opinion, the identification of originator *(auctor)* and author in such essays on the history of dogma appears to be arrived at somewhat too quickly and too smoothly. In fact, it is possible when considering a book to speak of an originator in a sense which is different from that of literary authorship. The concept of inspiration would then have to be distinguished from both these senses. Theoretically this is

tures is a real literary originator, a real author.[3] It is here that we
find a first approach to our problem. The human authors of
the Scriptures are not secretaries merely taking down divine
dictations; nor are they secretaries who, by their own intelligent
understanding and free will, receive whatever is illuminated
and presented by God. They are real originators and authors.
We may even say that they are authors in no less a sense

acknowledged in most of the usual treatises, but it seems to me that in
historical studies this distinction is not sufficiently remembered. If there is
also a prophetic inspiration, we should really have to investigate more
throughly whether we mean by the inspiration of Scriptures the inspired
character of many historical texts in the Fathers of the Church. What is
meant there is prophetic inspiration, which does not claim authorship,
though it includes a certain original right to the writings in which
prophetic inspiration is to be found. On the other hand, clearer ideas
about how theological concepts came about will show that the concept
of authorship as it exists in our experience cannot be applied to God
without modifications and deductions. Let us but think of the special
literary character of any writing and its relationship to the intellectual
stature of the author, by which the concept of authorship is usually
codetermined. This certainly could not be applied to God, since he is,
indeed, also linked with the literary form of the Holy Scripture in a
relation of originatorship, but not of authorship. We cannot here enter
any further into all these points. We also want to leave open the problem
whether the usual emphasis, deriving from Franzelin (that we are dealing
with literary authorship, and that this concept is more specific than originatorship, for example, of an authoritative kind, also with respect to
books) is merely an explanation of the dogma of God as the originator
of the Scriptures; or whether this view means anything beyond what may
simply pass for defined truth. For our purposes we simply assume that
God is the literary author of the Scriptures.

[3] See A. Bea, *De Scripturae Sacrae inspiratione* (Rome, 2nd ed. 1935), n. 37
(pp. 41 et seq.); S. Tromp, *De Sacrae Scripturae inspiratione* (Rome,
3rd ed. 1936), p. 55. The magisterial statements of the Church also speak
without any hesitation of men as the real authors of the Holy Scriptures.

than men usually are in regard to their own writings.[4] ⸀
divine authorship is neither a rival nor a diminuition of hum
authorship, which is not to be limited or reduced to a secretar
function. The mental picture of the "instrumentality" of ⸀
human author, which is frequently stressed in the teachi.
statements of the Church, must not be misunderstood in th
sense. It is precisely not a question of the instrumentality
a secretary in regard to the author, but of a human authorsh
which remains completely and absolutely unimpaired, which
permeated, embraced, but not diminished, by the divir
authorship. Only in this sense is it an "instrument" of Go
And it is an instrument in such a way that the instrumental⸀
of the writer, linked with the divine authorship, does not or
tolerate but also demands the human authorship, and that th
would be no point in divine authorship if man were but
secretary.

We shall certainly not be able to say that the usual descriptio

[4] In that respect according to my knowledge we do not have an
statement from the teaching authority of the Church. Still, by using th
analogy of our faith (indeed in anti-monophysitic and anti-monotheleti
fashion) and referring to Christ himself (remembering the well-know
analogy between the incarnation in the flesh and in the word), we ma
state that the free spontaneity of Christ's humanity was not lessened b
the divine person to whom this human nature belonged; not even thoug
this humanity was first established in a supreme and unparalleled manne
in the person of the Logos (cf. K. Rahner, *Schriften zur Theologie,*
[Einsiedeln, 1954], pp. 169–222, *passim*). In a similar fashion the sam
thing happens in the case of the writers if they are authors (which w
assume) and not just secretaries. They will then be authors no less, bu
even more so, than they would be in the natural case of human author
ship. Inspiration does not restrain what is man's own, but frees it;
implies no act of unimaginable compromise, but an application of th
basic relationship between God and man: both dependence from Gc

14

inspiration, by means of which God becomes the author of
e Scriptures, also clearly states that man remains, and must
main, an author.[5] In fact, we are led to believe that inspira-
on, as it is described, would be the more perfect if man were
ut a secretary. In any case, the actual customary description
oes not clearly exclude the merely secretarial function of the
uman writer; it would fit that function equally well. Further-
1ore, how can we conceive of two literary authors working
ogether, not in a team, but in such a way that each of them
vould be the author of the whole (*totalitate effectus* if not also
italitate causae)? In solving this difficulty, one cannot simply
efer to the transcendental character of the divine causality in
he running of the world and in co-operating *(concursus)* with
ts activities, where again two do the very same thing, although
rom different levels. For, if God is to be the literary author
of the Scriptures, he is, if we may formulate it in this way, a
:ategorical and not a transcendental cause. In other words, his
:ausality itself, and not only its effects, will be within the
limensions in which his creatures live and act. If he is to be the

ind full individuality grow in the created reality, as well as in the history
of redemption in even and not in reverse proportions.

[5] The Biblical Encyclical of Pius XII, *Divino afflante Spiritu,* emphasizes
oy right the writer's instrumentality in regard to God and concludes
:hat, therefore, the special character of the work could allow us to
:ecognize the human author and his special characteristics (*Ench. Bibl.,*
1. 556). This does not, however, answer our question. For it is obvious
:hat any instrumentality in the work will also reveal the peculiar nature
of the instrument. In that respect the special characteristics of Matthew,
Luke, etc. would be recognizable (in some way at least) even if they had
oeen only knowing and freely consenting secretaries.

Conversely the instrumentality of the human originator has to be
:onsidered and interpreted in such a way that it should not only explain

15

literary author of the Scriptures, and not only their transcendental cause – which in itself would not be sufficient for a literary authorship – then God must be at work within the redemptive dimension of the world, just as in the prophetic inspiration and in the miracle of the Incarnation, both representing activities of God's miraculous character; in a certain sense they in themselves, as actions of God and not only in their effects, possess a spatio-temporal determination. But as God in these cases is the person who originally spoke and acted alone, in the same way we cannot conceive of God otherwise than as the one and only author, who suffers no one else beside himself. This precisely because he is an "author" in that very dimension (otherwise he could only be originator, but certainly not author), in which man is living. Otherwise two kinds of authorships would have to exist in the same dimension. In other words, the same work from the same angle can have but one cause.[6]

the literary special characteristics of the writings themselves, but also that in every accuracy and literalness these human originators are not only secretaries of God but real human authors, even though because of the simultaneous divine authorship, they must be called *auctores secundarii*. This title does not imply a lessening of their authorship, but its subordination to the divine, which does not weaken, but, on the contrary, makes human authorship all the more real and intensive: see also A. Bea, "Pio XII e le scienze bibliche" in: *Pio XII Pont. Max. Postridie Kalendas Martias, 1876–1956* (Rome, 1956), p. 71.

[6] It does not help to refer – as many authors seem to do – to the axiom of St. Thomas: *idem effectus totus attribuitur instrumento et principali agenti etiam totus* (S. c. G. III, 70) and to conclude from it that in our case also the human author could appropriate to himself the whole effect – the book – and therefore become its author, because he is only an instrument of God, the primary author. Whatever the exact meaning of the quoted axiom in St. Thomas may be (it is intended to illustrate the transcendent

Thus the Scriptures – and that is our question – could not have two literary authors from the point of view of the literary authorship. Let it be noted that we do not say that the same work could not have two authors, one divine and another human, but that we say: It cannot be that the causality of both should, from the outset, aim at a single literary authorship. In that case, a single effect would be caused under the same aspect by two causes, which is impossible.[7] But if, on the other hand, we merely say that the human author is only instrumentally an author, we would have to explain why he does not thereby cease to be a real author (for an instrumental function in the composition of a writing for somebody else, who is the real author, is by definition, a secretarial function), and why it is that the role of the human author is not at least mini-mized, which, neither *a posteriori* nor *a priori,* appears to be feasible.

causality of God), it cannot apply here. If it were applicable, there could not be any mere secretary at all – since any secretary of God would, by virtue of this interpretation of the axiom, automatically become an author – and this goes also for the pen used. It would have to be the author of the book which was written by it as an instrument.

[7] This difficulty is naturally realized in theology. In order to meet it, reference is made to the doctrine on the relationship between God and acting creature in regard to concurrence. But it is not sufficiently clearly realized that, in the case in question, we have to explain precisely that which does not exist in concurrence, namely that through the subordi-nation of the causality of creatures to the divine causality, the latter takes on the effect of both. Because this is completely excluded in the general relationship between the action of the creatures and the con-currence of God, the literary individuality of various writings is, more-over, insufficiently explained if we were to say that God dealt with his instrument in such a way that it would act *d'une façon libre et personelle* (P. Benoit in A. Robert - A. Tricot, *Initiation Biblique* (Paris, 3rd ed.,

17

If this difficulty is not to remain unanswered, God obviously must be in one sense author of the Scriptures,[8] which should, firstly, leave unimpaired an authorship of the true, if analogical kind, while at the same time not being the same sense in which man is an author, and, secondly, would require and not merely tolerate the presence of a human author.

2. Some Problems Concerning the Concept of Inspiration

We have already shown how inspiration, which is to explain God's authorship, is being interpreted according to the traditional view. This interpretation is not to be contested. But we also said that, while strictly speaking, this interpretation treats of inspiration justifiably as a formal abstraction, it is in practice exposed to the danger of being given a certain meaning, which is by no means necessarily part of the dogmatic aspect of inspiration. We shall have to elucidate this further, because we shall thereby attain a new formal lead for our quest of the right material meaning of the concept of the inspiration. Everyone who, in connection with the explanation of inspiration, is told about the illumination of the intellect and the motivation of the will by God, will instinctively imagine something, and he may be entitled but not compelled to do so. There have been many theologians who have held that inspiration by no means implied basically a communication of hitherto unknown matters, even less so an infusion of images. Indeed, according

1954, p. 17). For that would also be the case when the "instrument" was but a secretary.

[8] The "sense" is meant in a real-ontological and not only gnoseological sense, *per se* and not *quoad nos* (only).

to them, the human author need not be at all conscious of it as being distinct from the prophetic inspiration.[9]

But what about the "illumination" of the intellect? As this word is normally understood, an illumination which communicates nothing, or even remains unconscious, is no illumination at all.[10] We may, of course, say that the content is thereby

[9] Cf. M. Nicolau, *Sacrae Theologiae Summa,* i (Madrid, 2nd ed. 1952), p. 1005; B. Mariani, "Ispirazione" in: *Enciclopedia Cattolica,* vii (Rome, 1951), p. 324: "Non è necessario che l'agiografo sia consapevole della sua ispirazione"; Lercher-Schlagenhaufen, *Institutiones theol. dogm.,* i (Innsbruck, 1939), n. 568 (pp. 345 et seq.); P. Benoit, op. cit., p. 16 (Caiphas was able to prophesy the death of Jesus [John 11:51] without knowing of it). Lercher Schlagenhaufen commented: "Communiter tamen assumitur, de facto hagiographos conscientiam inspirationis habuisse", and refers to Suarez, *De fide,* disp. 8, sect. 4 in: *Vives* xii, pp. 232ff. Whether or not this reference to Suarez is valid, we do not wish to decide here. St. Thomas appears, "with greater probability" not to have held consciousness to be a necessary element of inspiration, as Bea, *De inspiratione* (Rome, 2nd ed. 1935), n. 52, writes. In any case, we may state with Bea (loc. cit.): "Recentiores auctores plerique partem negativam tenent." Bea quotes on behalf of the claim for a consciousness of inspiration S. M. Zarb alone among modern authors: "Num hagiographi sibi conscii fuerint divinae inspirationis" in: *Angelicum,* ii (1934), pp. 228–44. It would be, in fact, rather difficult to see how an opinion about their inspiration, expressed by hagiographers is also to accord with the form of their expressions: in Luke 1:1 et seq.; 2 Cor. 7:8; 2 Mach. 15:38 et seq.; "Here then I will make an end of my writing; if it has been done workmanlike and in historian's fashion, none better pleased than I; if it is of little merit, I have done as well as I could."

[10] Naturally one can object by arguing that a deepening of our capacity to judge and of the judgement concerning the sentences to be written, are an "illumination" (cf. Bea, op. cit., n. 45–9: "Haec motio in eo consistit, quod Deus . . . intellectum hagiographi ita tangit, ut hac motione elevatus iudicia in libro exprimenda eliciat; simul ipsa objecta in clariore luce ponuntur et facultas intellectiva maiorem accipit optentiam illuminativam maiusque robur, ut haec iudicia sint vera et

illuminated which is already there and adds to our confidence in regard to it. It may be said that such an illumination need not in itself be conscious, nor conscious as an actual inspiration, though perhaps it hovers on the borderline of consciousness. However, even so the question still remains whether an inspiration thus circumscribed would make any difference to the authorship of God.[11] And yet the theologians are right who

certa ea veritate et certitudine, quae est cognitiones divinae: 2. 2. q. 171, a. 6"); but the question is still this – what is the effect of such an illumination upon the book itself? If we could imagine an "illumination" which, without adding any new elements to the knowledge, nevertheless increases the firmness of the judgement (which is by no means clear) there still remain the questions: a. has not this "illumination" to be conscious after all, or how could a *clarior lux,* a brighter light, remain unconscious? This needs at least some explanation, though we do not argue that such a "light" ought to have an object-consciousness and be liable to perception. But a completely unconscious "light of the spirit" is surely a contradiction in itself: b. how does the illumination affect the work more than some purely negative assistance? This certitude granted by the illumination can affect the written sentences, it would seem, only if there is in them some meaning which can but be put into writing, and which would otherwise not exist. But illuminated certitude makes sense in regard to authorship only if it affects the work itself, and not merely the mental condition of the author. Nor can it be simply stated that the concept of inspiration necessitated by the sources of the faith requires such illumination, even when a certain thus necessary element has no bearing on the actual authorship. For the sources of the teaching office of the Church derive authorship from the very act of inspiration: because it is inspired, God must be the author; c. why does such illumination make for authorship or why is such illumination required beyond the prophetic inspiration, (which, after all, is directly or indirectly apparent in all the books of the Bible), although as such it seems to have no relevance for the authorship as such (in other words, we wonder whether the sources really postulate such an illumination?).

[11] An illumination in that sense would be more of a subsidiary help

speak of the unconsciousness of inspiration, despite considering illumination as characteristic of it. There are many, weighty reasons which show that the formal concept of inspiration, taken in itself and in a general sense, does not contain a change of consciousness of which the human author need be aware. "Illumination" here can only mean that God acts effectively in such a way that the human author's reason receives a certain sure knowledge willed by God, and only this alone. It remains an open question how God achieves this, whether through a psychological change of the spiritual process, of which the author will become conscious, or in some other manner, which could be conceived in very different ways. Obviously, it is sufficient that the effect is attained. The human author perceives something because God effectively wills him to do so

in announcing the content of some knowledge, giving it written form, rather than a matter through which one would become the author of knowledge thus illuminated. In objection it may again be suggested that illumination as a factor in God's authorship implies the connection with the motioning of the writer's will by God, and that the illumination in itself without this motioning would not suffice to make God an author (which had not been claimed). Again we reply by asking, what is then the meaning of this illumination (even in connection with the motioning of the will) for God's authorship, unless in itself it has to make some meaningful contribution? In order to cut short the discussion, it may of course be claimed that tradition has, after all, always understood inspiration in this way, and that we must take these positive sources into account, regardless of whether their statements can be derived from the concept of literary authorship or not. Again we may reply by asking whether these positive sources do actually propose this, as matter beyond any dispute, or whether they merely use such images in order to clarify the essentials, namely, that God is the author of the Holy Scriptures, and that such images need not be regarded as articles of faith? Moreover, are the restrictions of the concept of illumination (unconsciousness, etc.) which, without contradiction, are

21

by such a will, which is not only permissive, passive and co-operative, but also predetermining, in scholastic terminology a *predeterminatio formalis*.[12]

On the actual motioning of the will in inspiration many, though not all, theologians hold[13] that it can quite well

imposed on the traditional concept of illumination in the older sources, also covered by the positive sources of faith?

[12] That this aspect of the effective, formal predefinition in itself is not sufficient, though necessary in order to make God an author, will have to be discussed in some other connection. Here it might be noted that the theologians rightly point to the analogy between inspiration and actual, efficient grace. The Molinists at least among these theologians would have to agree that the element of efficiency in actual grace, which is the point of the analogy, need not be contained in some special mark of grace through which it becomes "interior" grace. What is required for the efficiency of grace (as distinct from merely sufficient grace) may depend on some extrinsic circumstances, which, according to the Molinists, has been foreseen by God through his *scientia media,* foreseen and willed by him as material to man's decision. Why should we not assume this also to be the case in inspiration, both in regard to the divine influence on human reason and on the human will? For it is, in fact, this absolutely willed efficiency of the influence, that is, a predefining efficiency that is required for God to be the author of the Scriptures. Also with regard to the sources we may ask whether the concept of an interior efficiency of inspiration, inasmuch as such a concept should be attested by the sources, is a statement about the matter itself, or only a manner of speaking, by which is to be meant no more than that God has a predefining efficient influence on the origins of Scripture.

[13] Cf. Lercher-Schlagenhaufen, op. cit., n. 565: "Motio voluntatis potest concipi ad modum influxus immediate physici in voluntatem . . . sed motio voluntatis, ut videtur, eodem modo explicari poterit per influxum divinum mediatum: . . . sive mediante impulsu externo (cf. *iussione divina:* Apoc. 1:10; Is. 8:1; Jer. 30:1, 2, *vel iussione angelorum:* Apoc. 19:9 et seq.); Immo potest Deus ex absoluta intentione libri perficiendi causas externas (preces aliorum) per specialem providentiam supernaturalem ita dirigere, ut hagiographus reapse scribere velit.

be reconciled with the view that the divine act does not affect the author's human will immediately from within, but by means of impulses, which are within the realm of the author's experience. This again is a conception which shows the strictly formal aspect of the traditional description of inspiration, and the danger of investing it with psychological, material meaning. Such a by no means certain interpretation will be dangerously close to mythology, if not to the confusion between the inspiration of the Scriptures and the prophetic inspiration of the human agent of a revelation which is new in content. Provided, therefore, that it is God's absolute will, he can also accomplish the motioning of the writer's will by causing him to be asked through other people to produce such writings. These requests and their realization will have to be, however, as we already observed, themselves matters of a divine, formal predefinition.

Thus the question, "how does God become the real author of the Scriptures?" yields the counsel not to overlook the formal character of the doctrinal teaching on inspiration and not to furnish it with meaning, which in some cases might be right *de facto,* but which cannot be postulated generally *a priori* wherever divine inspiration occurs.

If we now summarize the result of our two initial investigations, we may say this: an activity is required of God which, while making him the literary progenitor, nevertheless not

Motio voluntatis defert a gratia, quae datur ad modum actus supernaturalis indeliberati: haec enim per se non infallibiliter movet ad actum salutarem, illa infallibiliter movet ad scribendum." Nicolau (op. cit., n. 96, 97) holds the opposite view (basing himself on Bea) to be a more probable one only. This is, therefore, an open question among theologians. The same can also be said (under the same pre-suppositions) concerning the influence of the inspiring God upon the writer's mind.

23

only tolerates human authorship, but positively calls for this and is also formally different from it. Such an activity of God basically can be imagined in any manner, provided only that it but conceives,[14] will, and accomplishes the book by formal predefinition.

3. How the Church Knows the Scriptures to be Inspired

We now approach a third problem, which is to give us a hint of the right and adequate understanding of inspiration. How can the Church know, we ask, which books are inspired? We shall confine our initial discussion to the New Testament,[15] and concentrate on the Church, not on individuals, because we here assume it as proved, that this can be known by individuals univocally and clearly only through the Church and her teaching. That implies, however, that the objective indications in the Scriptures themselves do not allow of such a certain judgement to be made by the individual concerning their inspired character and, therefore, their canonicity. But what about the Church? How does the Church know it? This cannot be established, it seems, from the books themselves. It is not likely, at least not in most cases, that the authors themselves

[14] To "conceive" we must repeat, is taken in the sense, that God "conceives" this book also *as* book, as the mental manifestation and objectivation of the human author. Let us note what Benoit (op. cit., p. 31) says: "Dieu ne saurait être auteur à la façon d'un homme; lui attribuer des 'idées' qu'il communique à un secrétaire . . . est un anthropomorphisme, qui ne peut que fausser la recherche."

[15] We shall come back later to the question whether the results of our considerations reached in regard to the New Testament are applicable also to the problem of the inspired character of the Old Testament.

have referred to it, for we cannot even assume *a priori* that they themselves knew it. Is it, for instance, historically imaginable that St. Paul himself would have declared that his note to Philemon was inspired, claiming for it the rank and status of the Old Testament, or that St. Luke would have done the same in regard to his writings, compiled from sources and diary-notes which he had laboriously collected? And even if they had been able to testify concerning their own inspiration, it still has to be shown that they, in fact, did so and that their testimony was duly handed down, and it still has to be demonstrated why and on what grounds we should or must give credence, in the case of those who were not apostles, to their subjective impressions that they were inspired. And yet the inspiration of various writings is part of the revealed truths, which are entrusted to the Church only for custody (she could not multiply them). They must have been assigned to the Church before the death of the last apostle and cannot have been revealed at a later date. Moreover, they cannot have been revealed in some other statement, that is to say, implicitly, in a purely logical sense. For it is impossible even to conceive of a more universal statement from which it could be deduced or developed that, for example, the Epistle to Philemon is inspired. Or are we, in

We are entitled to proceed methodically in this way (although inspiration is formally the same in both Testaments) because it will be seen later that, in fact, a final recognition of inspiration and ultimate acknowledgement of the Canon is possible only in the New Testament. In other words, the Sacred Scriptures of the Old Testament were inspired because and inasmuch as the Old Testament is the preparation for the fullness of time. The nature, fact and extent of inspiration can, therefore, be understood definitely and univocally from the New Testament alone.

order to get over the difficulty, to lay down that everything written by an apostle must be inspired? Even if such a statement is more valid than it is generally believed to be,[16] questions remain which the theologians are unable to answer satisfactorily. For how are we to prove this statement? How could it be shown historically (if it is not to be deduced from another statement) always to have been a statement of the faith of the Church? Is it that the Pauline epistles were also inspired and did have God as their author? Can God, too, write works which may in substance be lost? And what about the writings

[16] Later we will show what is true in this idea. It certainly draws attention to a truth. But, this truth has to be proved, for it is not immediately evident that an apostle has to be inspired always, nor that an apostle alone can have been inspired. It has to be shown precisely why there is an intrinsic connection between apostleship and inspiration, of which tradition has always, if not explicitly, been aware. The fact that we do not possess any writing from an apostle which would not be acknowledged by the Church as inspired also points towards this connection. Is that a mere fact in the knowledge of the Church? The Epistle of Barnabas in spite of Tertullian (*De pudic.*, 20) and St. Jerome (*De viris illustribus,* 6) cannot serve as a positive answer to our question. What Pesch, Dorsch, Bea, Nicolau have to say against this ascribes a distinction to the statements of the Fathers which was alien to their minds. The statements of the Fathers in any case do not suggest that they were reckoning with the existence of apostolic writings which were not inspired. By the way, if we carry the argument further concerning the difference between Synagogue and Church in respect of their indefectibility we cannot equate the apostles of the Church with the prophets of the Old Testament, as though, if all writings of the apostles are inspired, this would also be valid *a priori* for all the writings of the prophets which they might have written. Concerning the literature on this question see the references in Bea (loc. cit.), Perrella in *Divus Thomas,* 35 (Piacenza, 1932), p. 51, and Nicolau (loc. cit.) on Ubaldi, Schanz, Jouon, Zarb, M.-J. Lagrange, Durand holding one view and Pesch, Dorsch, Bea, Ogara, etc. another.

of Mark and Luke, who were only disciples of the apostles? We are not entitled, after all, to declare *a priori* without further demonstration everything as canonical that came from men who were not apostles. It does not help much to say that whatever the apostles approved of in their disciples' work is their own writing and consequently – assuming the above-mentioned claim that all apostolic writings are inspired – also the writings of these apostolic disciples would be as inspired as apostolic writings. For there is no kind of approval of writings by means of which one could become an author.[17] Concerning the writings of Luke we shall have to hold that their author is very clearly not Paul, but Luke.

In order to avoid the dilemma, it is argued that the apostles or one apostle (perhaps the last one in the Church), had left behind a formal and explicit revelation on the inspired nature of the New Testament writings *in individuo,* in some statement which directly expressed this revelation. But is it historically probable that this did happen? Is it probable that, for example, one apostle did not know of his own inspired work in the case of certain smaller writings (e.g., the Epistle to Philemon) but that another apostle did receive an explicit categorical revelation concerning the inspiredness of the same writing? If Paul himself did not know of the inspiredness of at least some of his epistles (because they were short private letters; Philemon; Rom.

[17] If we were to argue, however, that the apostles had acknowledged the written records of Mark or Luke in some qualified manner, that they had become their own work (a possibility that cannot be excluded *a priori*) then consequently we would have to conclude that these writings, inasmuch as they were inspired, were not the writings of Mark or Luke? This would be contrary to the whole of tradition, which has always considered them as "evangelists" and inspired authors.

16:1–23), it is difficult to believe that there was another apostle (which one?) who himself certainly knew these epistles and would even testify to their inspiredness.

We have so far completely excluded the history of the Canon. How can we explain historically that the canonical or uncanonical (thus, what is inspired and what is not inspired) quality of many writings remained uncertain for a long time, if their canonical or uncanonical character through a formal and explicit statement of one of the apostles before his death must have been known to the Church as a revealed truth? Was, in fact, the real history of the Canon such that a writing was acknowledged as canonical and inspired – even if slowly – because there was found an explicit testimony in this sense, not only from apostolic times, but even from an apostle? Or rather because certain writings from apostolic times were recognized really to have originated at the time of the Church that is, to have been composed by one apostle and/or representing the original faith of the Church?[18]

[18] In contrast to the inspired canonical books, "apocryphal" in the times of the early Fathers does not mean "not having" God as the inspiring author, the authorship of which will be revealed if it exists but "in reality not by the apostle to whom it is ascribed, and contrary to the teaching of the Church, although originating more or less in the first generation of the Church": we mean simply a book, "which in fact, does not belong to the Apostolic Church". And the original sense of the term "canonical" too is mainly "to serve the rules of faith and morals (in contrast to writings which are against the revelation or outside of it) and *therefore* accepted into the list of such writings". We thus get a distinction between material and formalized canonicity. The latter is simply inspiredness, recognized and acknowledged by the Church; a book is canonical because it is acknowledged by the Church as inspired, and it is so acknowledged, because the Church knows that it is inspired. The former term "canonical" implies simply the recognition and acknowledgement that a book is "apostolic", that is to say, written by an apostle

But if the second hypothesis corresponds rather to the historical diagnosis of the development of the Canon, how can it be harmonized with what we have to hold as of faith about inspiration and canonicity? Implied are the truths, that there has been no subsequent inspiration and that the inspiredness of a certain writing is part of the truths revealed to the Church and, therefore, could not have been revealed later than in the apostolic generation. These questions are not to be answered at this stage. What is to be made clear for the present is that we do need a material content for the concept of inspiration which can answer these questions freely and without too many hypotheses that are historically unverifiable. Inspiration has to be conceived of in such a manner that it demonstrates by itself how the Church knows the inspiredness of the books of the New Testament, without the necessity of having recourse to any statement about it in apostolic times that has no historical support. Although canonicity and the inspiredness of the Scriptures must not be conceptually identified, it will, nevertheless, be advantageous to approximate these two concepts in their mutual relations in order to understand that the factual elements of the original, not as yet formalized canonicity, apply

and/or is an authentic expression of the faith of the Church of the apostolic generation. Inspiration is not used by the material concept of canonicity in order to determine its explicit and formal content. It can, therefore, be easily recognized in any book authorized by the Church, in any case more easily than the fact of inspiration as such, which could only be known by an explicit testimony of an apostle, and that is, historically speaking, highly improbable. Of course, it has to be shown why it is legitimate to conclude from the material concept of canonicity that there has been inspiration and that it can be recognized from that concept. To show this is the object of the second part of our paper.

29

to the inspired writings only. The recognition of canonicity in fact means to know inspiredness, without anyone knowing anything explicitly about a formal inspiredness, in order to recognize canonicity.

4. The Inspiredness of the Scriptures and the Teaching Authority of the Church

Now to a fourth problem, which can provide a pointer towards the correct and adequate understanding of inspiration. This is the relationship between inspired and canonical writing on the one hand and the teaching authority and tradition on the other. It has been said that the Church has involved herself in an insoluble contradiction over this problem. It is, of course, and rightly, one of the favourite arguments of Catholic apologetics against the Protestant idea of the Bible and the Church that the Scriptures cannot be their own authority, that they would be subject to human whim and could hardly be relevant and absolutely binding to our own historical situation, unless there was a living teaching authority to interpret them and apply their message to any new situation. From this point of view, the familiar Catholic explanation in regard to the relationship between the Bible and Church has an easy run. It starts with the pre-supposition of the Bible and shows that it needs an authority in order to fulfil its rôle as the living word of God for all men of all times. But, in fact, this relationship has not been adequately dealt with. For it can be argued, as it is argued by Protestant theologians, that the Church fixes the Canon of the Holy Scriptures and testifies to their inspiration. She does this by virtue of a teaching authority which claims and must claim infallibility for itself, if the books are to become really canonical, an absolute rule for faith and theology. If the authority is not canonical in this sense, then the Bible cannot be so either.[19] However, if the Church (as the official teaching organ) testifies for the Scriptures in their absolutely binding, canonical and ultimately inspired quality, she seems to involve herself in a contradiction. For either she weakens her own binding, "infallible" teaching authority, which she needs in support of the Scriptures, or she weakens the Bible in favour of the teaching authority at that moment when she testifies to this authority. For in this latter case, when she refuses to give up her own authority in favour of the Bible, she subjects the Scriptures to her authority of interpretation, as it is she who decides what the Scriptures really say and what they are permitted to say. To sum up, what is the point of an infallible teaching authority, if there is an infallible Bible? What is the point of an infallible Bible if there is an infallible authority? If there is an infallible teaching authority, then it is certainly in a position, quite independently from a Bible, infallibly to select from the stream of opinions and of human tradition (at the beginning of which we have the oral tradition of the Christian events), what has

[19] However, if we surrender in regard to both (in order to extricate ourselves from this difficulty) such a traditional, binding character which Protestants ascribe to the Bible, and Catholics to the Bible *and* the Church, then we shall, whether we like it or not, depart from the grounds of historical Christianity. Everything that is really Christian in faith and doctrine would be but the always new "event" which has no absolutely binding, unique origin in some determined spatio-temporal situation, where the redemption did happen once for all time. The Scriptures in that case would come about only through faith.

been revealed by God, and to proclaim it to the world.[20] What would be the point of an infallible Bible in the hands of an authority, which, in the Catholic Church did not always, even in her infallible decisions, rely upon the Scriptures, if it could also testify to the divine revelation unerringly without the Bible? If we answer the former objection by saying that the Scriptures cannot be their own interpretation, and, therefore, need an infallible interpretation, the Bible can claim no priority before the rest of tradition, since both would then need the teaching authority in the same way, so that the real meaning of the revelation shall be unerringly perceived from both. The Bible would then be as little capable as tradition of fulfilling its ultimate purpose of imparting God's truth to men, without an authority superior to both, which, again, could perform the same task by itself without the support of the Scriptures. If an infallible authority exists, then the Bible would have no specific function which could not equally well be performed without it. Thus, it is argued, we have to face the dilemma that, if we decide for the Bible, we do not know where to find its binding character; if we decide for the authority of the Church, we can hardly maintain authoritative writings beside it.

We thus get the opinion that we must find a compromise which would save the rivalling authorities by separating them from each other in time: in the time of the Apostolic Church we are to stick to tradition, the oral testimony of salvation through Christ, which, like all prophetic messages, has authoritative character. This testimony is, however, expressed in the

[20] It should be noted that this presupposition has been commonly made in Catholic theology since Bellarmin. We intend to show later that it is not a safe presupposition.

32

Scriptures so univocally and completely that tradition is being replaced, as it were, by its own secondary form. After the time of the Apostolic Church we have one teaching authority alone, fully and clearly subordinated to the Bible, dependent on it and with as much authority (whenever really important decisions are at stake), as is supported by the Bible. But individual protests against any decisions of the Church by appeals to the Scriptures are possible. The individual member of the Church of the present time can always appeal to the Church of the future, which might know more about the Bible.

Naturally we could brush aside the whole difficulty by reaffirming that it has pleased God to grant to the Church an infallible teaching authority, as well as an inspired, holy and unerring book, and that God himself would take care, through the Holy Spirit, which is active in the Bible and Church, that neither should contradict each other. Again, we can answer that, although it is right that the Church could get along without the Scriptures by relying only on her infallible teaching office, this still cannot exclude the fact that God has granted her inspired books, as it were, as an additional (though, in itself, not necessary) help for the better performance of her proper function. As the spirit of God guides and enlightens her teaching, so it is said, it need not be feared that it would ever violate the Bible. It would always understand the Scriptures in the very sense in which they were written. Consequently we would be wrong to maintain that a teaching authority would necessarily damage the authority of the Bible, even though it seemed to hold that there is no absolute need for the Bible, inasmuch as the authority of the magistracy is more independent, extensive (in regard to, the content of the teaching), and more direct (in regard to the

33

individuals to be taught), than the authority of the Bible. We do not dispute this argument, at least not in its general tenor. We shall show later that some qualifications are needed. We would also agree that, on the level of apologetics, this answer is quite adequate. But it seems to us a rather dangerous theological positivism to suggest that it has pleased God to give his Church two infallible authorities, even if one of them would have been sufficient; and that there is no more to be said about it, because this is God's free decision which we have but to accept. For, by foregoing a more specific relationship between Bible and teaching authority simply because they exist, without there being any common objective root (except that both are established by God), and, therefore, without intrinsic relationships and mutual reference to each other – we shall be faced with the question whether we do not thereby dispense the dogmas of the Church from that measure of meaning without which in the long run, and for the multitude of men, the belief in them would be little more than an abstract possibiliy. A positivism of this kind might have the vestiges of a humble and prudent faith, since it is averse to "speculations" of any kind. Ultimately, however, it creates in men a feeling of the improbability of what is but positively laid before them and leads to unbelief.

Naturally, it is not possible, either at this stage or anywhere else in our treatise, to give an all-round answer to this problem. We would have to deal at length with the teaching authority and the Church in general. But one other question deserves to be mentioned, not in order to discuss it in full, but to demonstrate the extensive range of the problem of inspiration. For if one single theological problem can stir up the whole of theology, we may be sure that it has been correctly asked. Our problem relates to the sufficiency of the Bible. It might be assumed that, as far as Catholic theology is concerned, it is already settled that tradition (and the teaching authority on which it is based), constitute a material source besides the Bible which the Catholic faith cannot do without. Consequently, the relationship between the Scriptures and the teaching authority must be defined so loosely as to account for this tacitly assumed fact. For if the teaching authority, following upon the Apostolic Church, derives its teachings from two different sources, and in such a manner that the "oral tradition" contains elements not to be found in the Bible, the mutual relationship between teaching authority and tradition cannot, naturally, be so close as to establish between them a relationship of mutuality in which both of them would be but two elements of the same nature, constituting itself clearly in both. Theologians in recent centuries have been accustomed to regard tradition and Scripture as two material sources for the teaching authority of which the "oral tradition", even after the completion of inspired and canonical Scriptures, may propose matters not contained in the Bible. This thesis was believed to have been proved by the teaching of the Council of Trent that Bible and tradition are to be accepted with equal respect in establishing the faith and the practice of the Church, and also by the indication that, without the "oral tradition", neither the inspiredness of the Bible, nor the range of canonical books could be known with certainty. At the same, this explanation was tacitly used as an example for very different cases. Today we realize that the Council of Trent made no decision at all in this sense. As regards the doctrine – as distinct from discipline – the Council declared in principle no more than that the teaching office of the living

35

Church is the possessor, custodian and authentic interpreter of Scriptures, and that the Two Sources Theory (to coin a phrase) is but a possible interpretation of the Council which is not supported by the unanimous opinion either of the Fathers, or of the mediaeval theologians. Moreover, it could never claim general consent in the post-Tridentine period, but remained only an opinion. If, furthermore, we consider the possibility that the necessity of testifying to canon and inspiration through oral tradition is not just one among many cases, but a unique phenomenon resulting from the relationship itself between Church and Scriptures and, therefore, not to be generalized, our problem will have a scope very different from that generally held. We are thus entitled to conceive this relationship in such a way that the Church, in order to be what God ultimately wishes her to be, necessarily establishes the Bible, therefore attesting it for all time as inspired, but, because the Bible has been created from the beginning as *the* Scripture of the Church, and has in this way emerged as inspired, the mind of the Church has been adequately realized in the Scriptures. Nevertheless, the Bible necessarily remains for ever enshrined by the knowledge of the Church that these particular Scriptures are her canonical and inspired books. This knowledge of the inseparable link between herself and the Bible, an existential connection, cannot become part of the content of the Scriptures. It is not, therefore, permissible to conclude that the Bible, on this account, cannot otherwise be capable of sufficiency in regard to its content, or at least, *de facto* not of such sufficiency. Just as in the case of a human act, the concomitant I-consciousness can never be replaced by an I-consciousness that has become the object of an act, and just as it cannot be concluded from this that there must be other cases which would fall outside the range of such an objective consciousness, so the Scriptures as the adequate objectivity of the primal consciousness of the Church can never be separated from her consciousness, never to be expressed in writings alone, that these are her writings. It cannot, however, be concluded from this that there must also be other matters in the faith-consciousness of the Church which are not contained, not even implicitly, in the Scriptures. We know that, up to the present day, even in dogmatic definitions which contain truths apparently remote from the Bible, the teaching authority always looks for the "biblical basis". It is not our business here to discuss how the theologian has to conceive of the connection between biblical statements and later defined statements of doctrine. Thus we can confidently contest, that, "outside" the truths of inspiration and of the Canon, it would be impossible to cite statements which are neither explicitly nor implicitly contained in the Bible, and are yet to be considered as truths of the faith. They derive from an "oral tradition", handed down to us as a second source in its own right besides the Scriptures. However, if both necessity and fact in this "Two Sources Theory" are disputed, it is possible to imagine the relationship between teaching authority and Bible to be so close as to allow for a far simpler solution than that proposed by theological positivism with its two entities – unerring Scripture and the teaching office.

We have, in certain points, anticipated our later considerations. What matters at this stage is but to realize that inspiration should be understood as demonstrating from its own nature that the Bible is *the* book (not any book), and *the* source for the teaching authority and, conversely, that the Scripture is, from the beginning, the book of the Church who can testify to its inspiration because it is her book. If such an intimation of the nature of inspiration is possible, we may hope for a solution to the question raised in this chapter. Whether our investigation of the relationship between teaching authority and Bible will result in a deeper understanding of inspiration must be left until later. Our arguments against the "Two Sources Theory" should not be understood, however, in a way as though the problem of the inspiration of the Bible could not be solved unless the "Two Sources Theory" were false. We intended but to indicate some more general questions linked with our problem and to suggest that in theology, the most uniform and simple solutions of particular questions may again depend on the right solution of another question.

We leave aside other problems that might come within our scope. We might have asked, for example, how it is that God could be the literary author of the various books without necessarily having to be the author of the specific literary style of the text concerned; how it is, for example, that God could be the literary author of the Epistle to Philemon without having to say that God himself wrote a letter to Philemon.

II

THE THESIS

HOW are we now to answer the questions emerging from our previous summary considerations? Our answer, in order to be brief, will have to proceed by means of synthesis. It can, therefore, not be developed from the problem raised, but by the simple and systematic establishment of a thesis, on the basis of which the answers to our questions will then emerge. We will begin with some theological statements.

1. God has Founded the Church

God wills the Church and has instituted her. His is an absolute will. He intends her to be, therefore, in redemptive-historical pre-definition. This partly because his design for the Incarnation of the Logos is an absolute one, and made by God prior to any human, free, decision, which could have been its motive. The Church is also implied in this design. Another reason is that the Church, as distinct from the Synagogue, is a Church for all time, the ultimate and irrevocable economy of salvation, the concrete representation of God's free, triumphant, unconditional design for our salvation. God does not, therefore, merely appropriate the Church for himself like other works generally of which he is the transcendent cause, and which consequently refer back to him as their author. There is a two-fold distinction between the authorship of God in regard to the Church on the one hand, and to all his works in "nature" on the other. The Church springs from an absolute will which precedes and yet includes the freedom of man. "Will" is used here, not only in the sense of a capacity to determine, but also as a determining act. All creation, inasmuch as it is originally planned by God, is also the result of such a will. But what is thus created is not as yet an act of creaturely freedom, but precedes it. However, if something comes into being which is a free act of man or results from it, and, nevertheless, is absolutely pre-defined by God, and thus miraculously delimited from the normal run of things,[21] we can no longer speak merely of the world as something willed by God, but must recognize that, within the world, at certain spatio-temporal points, there is some qualitatively

[21] Those who think that all actions of free creatures are formally predefined by God (disregarding how such predefinition may be conceived) necessarily will have to introduce this element of explicit prediction and of the historical statement miraculously predefined and not merely permitted into the concept of predefinition concerning the Church. This will be necessary in order to distinguish it properly from their propositions, which *ex supposito* exist everywhere. Indeed, wherever God formally predefines something through miraculous prediction and intervention, we get an appropriation by God of the predefined work, as this does not exist in the predefinitions of a free action by men, which remains undetermined in its moral quality whether it is ultimately good or bad, and is not predefined by God's miraculous action in the world. As we do not have to decide here whether a formal predefinition of man's free action is something normal or something extraordinary, we add this second condition for "safety's sake". Objectively, it does in any case exist in the institution of the Church and explains, even if it could be dispensed with, why the Church is God's work in a special sense, which God in a special sense appropriates through the manner of this intervention.

preferential will at work, the terminus of a divine action, having spatio-temporal distinctiveness within the world, and thus assigning this quality to the divine action itself. We have thus got an actual history of redemption as historical action on God's part, which appropriates its object and effect in a qualitatively higher fashion than any other works. In other words, the "works" of the history of redemption are God's in some other, higher way than the works of nature. In the latter, God deals with the (historical) world, in the former, he enacts his own history in the world.

Moreover, this historical action of God once again attains its unique climax in Christ and the Church. Before it was an action which appeared on the stage of the world – *olim loquens patribus in prophetis* – but reserved its possible withdrawal. This means that not only the final outcome of the dialogue between God and man (as seen from within the world) remained open before Christ, undecided whether it would end in judgement or grace, but the objective realizations of the divine action itself bore the possibility of frustration or revocation.[22] Examples are the destruction of the Synagogue through the rejection of Christ, and the nebulous character of the sacraments in the Old Testament

[22] From this angle precisely the positive peculiarity of the Old Testament writings can best be visualized. It is the reality of the Old Testament which remains because it is actually the only permanent, representative validity of the prehistory of Christ and of his Church. But we perceive also the negative aspect of the Old Covenant. The Word, as a positive law of God, valid and commanding obedience (and that was the original meaning of the Old Testament) is no longer valid in this sense. But this possibility was contained in the Law from the beginning. In that respect there is a contrast to the New Testament, both affirmed verbally and written with greater finality.

41

which could cease to be signs of grace. Both are no longer possible in Christ and in the Church. They are the definitive presence of God's grace in the world, an eschatological event of mercy, an end of history. We may say that, in the institution of the Church, God makes the Church his own in a unique fashion because it is the work, i. of his formal predefinition, as ii. a redemptive-historical predefinition, that is to say, iii. of an eschatological kind.

2. The Apostolic Church[23]

The Apostolic Church in a qualitatively unique manner is subject to divine intervention also as distinct from the preservation of the Church in the course of history.[24] The Apostolic Church (in the first generation) has a singular and irreplaceable function for all the rest of the history of the Church,[25] so that what has been said in the preceding section about the Church as instituted by God, applies to the Apostolic Church in a special way, and is valid for the Church of later ages essentially also because she is based upon the early

[23] The exact meaning of this theological concept is important for our purpose. For the moment it is used simply for the Church in the time of her foundation, in the first generation, in which she herself is still in the stage of growth.

[24] We do not wish to deny the many similarities between the intervention of God in the Apostolic Church and in the Church of the later periods. Mostly (and rightly) these similarities rather than the differences are emphasized.

[25] Cf. the more generally known modern literature, which, in the struggle for the primacy of Peter has investigated whether and to what extent Peter and the apostles enjoyed a special status which essentially cannot envisage successors: P. Gaechter, "Die Wahl des Matthias" in

Church. It is not as if a nature had not been posited with the institution of the Church, that is, a mission and power which, lasting through the ages, exists in each generation. Nevertheless, the first generation had a unique, irreplaceable function.

The Church in her God-willed nature, especially according to the Catholic view, is not merely an actuality, the ever-new event of the faith. Indeed, the Church has, as part of her divinely-given nature, an institutional character, which is what history is concerned with and is what endures in history. This implies a beginning in time and a continuation. That which comes later is based upon earlier events. Later events, in spite of their development and unfolding, always exist only because they derive from the given origin, the Apostolic Church, and not only from the originator, God. They derive from the foundations and not only from him who laid the foundation. This foundation, however, is not Christ alone, but the community which he himself has gathered round him, and on which he bestowed his spirit on the first Pentecost. The Apostolic Succession and the *paradosis* (of the content of the teaching and of the missions of Jesus, and of the foundation of the credibility of this message through the transmitted testimony of the resurrection) are elucidations of this fact. These phenomena do not merely suggest that something has been handed on and exists, therefore, also at a later date, but also that something will be handed on

Zeitschrift für katholische Theologie, 71 (1949), pp. 318–46 (especially pp. 318–33); E. Kredel, "Über den Apostelbegriff" in *Zeitschrift für katholische Theologie,* 78 (1956), pp. 137–68; A. Voegtle, "Der Petrus der Verheißung und der Erfüllung" in *Münch. Theol. Zeitschrift,* 5 (1954), pp. 1–47; O. Cullmann, *Die Tradition als exegetisches, historisches und theologisches Problem* (Zürich, 1954). It is obvious that this literature could not be discussed here.

because it was there earlier; because he who first passed it on had something to pass on, as well as the power to do so in such a way that everything that is to be later will always have to depend on there always having been something to hand on, and this power determines, both positively and negatively, the extent of later possibilities. God has, therefore, instituted the Church, not simply by keeping it in being for ever, but he keeps her in being also (if not, only!) by having instituted her once, at a particular moment in time. God, then, as the founder of the Church, has a unique, qualitatively not transmissible relationship to the first generation of the Church, which he has not in the same sense to other periods (or, rather, which he has to these only through the first). To contest this would be to deny implicitly that, for instance, revelation was terminated with the death of the last apostle, that Peter was not only the first pope and the apostles were not only the first bishops, but something more than that which, according to the Bible, was theirs in a unique and not transferable manner. The act of the institution of the Church is thus qualitatively different from that of her preservation. The theologians have expressed this by saying that, in regard to the permanently established nature, the preservation of the Church is an *assistentia per se negativa*. This, however, cannot be said of the institution as such. It follows that God made the Apostolic Church his own, having founded and not only having preserved her. Similarly, the act of being born and the act of living do not have, qualitatively, the same connection with the mother. The beginning, therefore, has an originality, a non-derivativeness and purity of essence, notwithstanding the necessity of a later unfolding, that are proper only to this first phase. Naturally, this does not mean that whatever follows is merely a human product, a Christian history of religion, a human theology and history of theology – instead of a history of the Church, dogmatics and history of the dogma as the God-given unfolding through the Holy Spirit of that divine originality itself. The Apostolic Church,[26] as the newly started beginning of the Church, which has yet to develop, is that, which, because still becoming, is not her own guide nor the governor of her course but, therefore, in a unique and eminent sense the work of God: *Deum habet auctorem*. Conversely, this Apostolic Church is not only the first period of the Church in time, but the permanent ground and norm for everything that is to come. It is the law according to which the whole course of the Church is being steered.

Naturally, two factors have to be remembered; i. this original institution itself has a duration measurable by physical time and is not just a single instant in time. We may simply say that it is the time of the first generation which, naturally, is not ended at a certain calendar-date unless we wish to say — (which would be meaningless) — that this first generation in our special sense ends on the day on which the last apostle died. Theologically speaking, we are not entitled to hold that the Church was already complete on the day of Pentecost. The Church indeed had visible existence as a community, a legal structure, at least in its basic traits, and the Holy Spirit. Still, she was not yet complete. There is, in fact, *L'Église naissante* in the literal sense of Batiffol's term, the Church about to be born, which has a

---

[26] By "Apostolic Church" we mean the time in which revelation was still subsiding as event (and not as tradition alone) and has yet to settle down, when the Church was yet to be, and not merely to remain, Church.

duration in time. In order to understand this point, let us remember that the Church, whose mission it is, as is rightly said, "but" to conserve and to interpret the revelation, did not exist as such at Pentecost. For there was revelation also after Pentecost, for instance about the Canon of the inspired writings. The Church having "only" that role was not yet there, because at that particular instant the Apostolic Church had both more and less than that task alone. She had yet to receive revelations anew, and she could not as yet guard and conserve all that she has today, because it was not yet revealed to her: ii. also in the case of this Apostolic Church during the period of her growth, we encounter phenomena which did not belong to her, to her realized nature, to the true possibilities of her autonomy, such as the quarrels in Jerusalem, the erroneous opinions in Thessaloniki and in Corinth, etc. As the Church, to the end of time and eschatology, she must have the capability of delimitating her own boundaries from alien phenomena, which, however, occurred within her. She could not otherwise be what she has to be – she would have lost her nature, would have been the Synagogue instead of being the Church.[27] This capacity for pure self-expression and clear and univocal delimitation against the pseudo-ecclesiastical and pseudo-Christian phenomena must have been possessed by the Apostolic Church, and by the Church

---

[27] This explains why there was not and could not be a closed, authoritative formation of the Canon of the same clarity in the Old Testament as we have it in the Church both for the Old and the New Testament. A synagogue, which may err cannot have the infallible capacity for distinguishing alien from essential elements as the Church has, which could not be alienated from the truth, because in the final stage of time of the irrevocable Incarnation of the Logos – *praedefinitione formali* – God no longer wills it. But we shall come back to this point later.

in regard to the Apostolic Church in a special measure. The Church must always have this capacity. Otherwise, she could in time be mistaken for her counterpart. She would then no longer be an historical fact as the visible representative of God's grace in Christ. She would merely continue to exist in "spirit", that is, in the world of ideals. This delimitation of herself must be supposed to have existed in a special measure in the primitive Church. For the existence of a Canon as an historical entity for the Church of all times means that the later Church is able relatively easily to continue this self-critical delimitation, because she can always refer to this Canon. For then we shall have norms that can be historically tested. The crucial question is thus the constitution of this Canon itself. Whether exact references to it are actually made later is an important, though, compared with the basic correctness of the Canon itself, a secondary matter. The faculty of the self-measuring self-possession has its unique point of culmination wherever the Church thus ruling and norm-giving emerges, rather than the Church looking for the norm and adapting herself to it. Of course, the formal teaching authority of the Church and the assistance of the Holy Spirit promised to her, can never replace the Canon of faith and morals of the Church. It is guaranteed to her teaching and pastoral office that it will be able to apply the norm correctly, but not that it will be able to judge the later phenomena without the norm of an objective-material and historically verifiable kind.

3. The Scriptures as Constitutive Elements of the Church

The Bible, too, belongs to the constitutive elements of this Apostolic Church as the qualitatively unique work of God and the permanent "canonical" origin for the later Church. "Too", because the essentially constitutive elements of the Apostolic Church must include everything that belongs to the Church in general, possession in faith of the handed-down revelation, the *ius divinum* of primacy and succession in the following of the apostles, sacraments, the social basis of the community, and much else which otherwise is proper to the Apostolic Church as such, to Peter, to the apostles and the function of both as true instruments of revelation. But the constitutive elements of the Apostolic Church also include the Scriptures, despite the priority of oral paradosis in the Apostolic, growing Church, which is prior to the Scripture according to the free, though objectively understandable will of God. This fact cannot be disputed. For there are Holy Scriptures, and they are essentially books of the Church to be recognized only through her as Scripture given to her, to be interpreted through her and thus to be actualized in their own nature through the Church. The Scriptures are part of the fully-developed essence of the Church, as her constitutive elements.

Yet some more precise qualifications are needed. Notwithstanding the fact that the Scriptures originate as God's word to man, they are just as genuinely[28] a self-expression of the faith of the Church, a written embodiment of that which the primitive Church believed and what in faith she laid down for herself. To deny this would be to deny the fact that the New Testament writers were real authors and would be to reduce them to mere

---

[28] This "just as genuinely" has to be explained in order to be justified. That means, it has to be shown why and how from the same material root the Scriptures can be both word of God and also self-declaration of the Church – and the one dependent upon the other.

transmitters of a message from above, which would contradict the actual character of these writings, and also contradicts their *genus litterarium* as a witnessing of the faith and not only a witness of revelation. What actually happened was not, of course, that in some way a book was composed *deo auctore,* and then later the same book was recognized by the Church as a letter from God to her, declared as authentic, and introduced as a textbook of the faith, newly imported from outside. The writings of the New Testament originate as life-processes of the Church; they are the sediments of that which in her has, been transmitted and preached as her faith; they are writings which come into existence as manifestations of communal life, as letters, exhortations, sermons, etc. Thereby the Scriptures have, from the start, – "originally" – also[29] that function which we generally attribute to the Apostolic, as distinct from the later Church. She is not only the first phase temporally, but also permanent source and Canon, the norm for the later Church. She is thus also because of the Scriptures. In this function of the primitive Church, the Scriptures are not some neutral factors introduced from outside, but part of this very function, inasmuch as the Church, her *paradosis,* her faith and self-realization are actualized in writing.[30] By thus forming the Scriptures in herself, she

---

[29] "Also" and not "not only".

[30] To write implies, of course, the intention of preserving and keeping for later. Even in ancient times writing was not merely a means of bridging separations in space, but also a link with the future. Otherwise there would have been no point in keeping what was written, or to use stone and similar durable materials unsuitable for transportation. We may safely assume similar intentions both in the writer and in the recipient who conserves the writing. The writer, too, has more than his own contemporaries in mind.

49

addresses herself as the norm-giving Apostolic Church towards her own future and, conversely, by establishing herself as the law for all times to come, she forms the Scriptures.[31] It is precisely in the formation of the Scriptures that the Church confirms that unique delimiting understanding of herself which is, as we said, hers in a particular degree, in order to become the "Canon" of the later Church.

4. The Thesis

If what has been said in the preceding section is correct, it follows that, in creating through his absolute will the Apostolic Church (cf. pp. 40-43) and her constitutive elements (cf. p. 48), God wills and creates the Scriptures in such a way that he becomes their inspiring originator, their author. Let it be noted that we say "creating", for we wish to stress that the Scriptures originate not only on the occasion, or in the course of the institution of the Apostolic Church, but that the active, inspiring authorship of God is an intrinsic element in the formation of the primitive Church becoming Church, and derives its marks from being this. God wills the Scriptures and himself as their originator. He achieves both because and in so far as he wills himself as the acting and efficient author of the Church. The inspiration of the Scriptures (naturally with the proviso of what

[31] We do not necessarily wish to maintain that the primitive Church deposited her entire "oral" *paradosis* in the Scriptures. But even those who disagree with this opinion can, nevertheless, accept our basic thesis. Whether the sufficiency of the Bible as material source (apart from its own testimony through the Church) is disputed by right, is another question. We have already suggested why this question is of some importance for the problem of the relationship between teaching office

was said in II, 3, p. 48), is but simply the causality of God in regard to the Church, inasmuch as it refers to that constitutive element of the Apostolic Church, which is the Bible.

5. Inspiration and Old Testament

We have not so far entered into the question of whether our proposed thesis could also explain the inspiration of the Old Testament. For reasons of method we have until now used data which referred primarily to the Church and to the New Testament. It could also be thought that the whole theory of inspiration might fail, since the Old Testament has also to be regarded as inspired in the same way as the New Testament. Yet our interpretation of inspiration could not be applied to the Old Testament. Therefore, either a different kind of inspiration has to be assumed for the Old Testament, which is impossible, or inspiration has to be denied, which would be heretical. We shall now have to deal with this objection.

Let us first consider some points which are usually overlooked. Although inspiration and canonicity are two conceptually and materially different matters, they are not, therefore, independent of each other. And this not only because canonicity presupposes inspiration of the book which attests for the Church. There is also a certain relation of mutual dependence.

and Bible and consequently for the nature of inspiration. It is not, however, decisive for our thesis of inspiration. But the relationship between teaching authority and Bible would be much simpler if we could assume that the tradition of the primitive Church – inasmuch as it is a univocally binding and real norm, valid also for the later Church – was reflected in Scripture. Our thesis would then become even clearer. But, as we said, this assumption is not necessary for our proposed opinion.

Inspiration exists fully when authentically attested, when the canonicity is recognized. God does not write books for himself alone. Whatever he writes is, necessarily, addressed to someone and makes sense only if it "arrives" when the writing is recognized as written by God with that certainty – which is necessary – in order that this writing should express validly its character as an authoritative word of God. Inspiration is thus meaningful only if canonicity is added to it.

The Synagogue did not, however, possess the same power as the Church, to be the infallible witness of the inspired nature of the Scriptures. There was no infallible teaching authority – not even before the death of Christ – in the Old Testament, in the sense of a permanent institution, which had this inerrant character. There were prophets every now and again. But there was no infallible Church. The "end of times", the last, definite act of redemption had not yet occurred. The Synagogue was capable of apostatizing from God and taking her official stand on the denial of God and Christ, thus abrogating for the future her own existence as God's foundation. This is not to say that, at the time of the Old Testament, there could have been no knowledge whatsoever about canonicity and inspiration of a book. That would not only contradict the fact that there were writings at the time which were acknowledged as inspired, but, even more significantly, that this Old Testament knowledge of a certain canonicity in itself was confirmed as materially and formally right by Jesus, the apostles and the Church. Just as there were prophets who were authorized by God to speak, and they attested their message awakening faith, so it was, of course, possible to have a knowledge, ultimately of prophetic character, of the inspiration of the Scriptures and their reference to the religious community of the Synagogue. We can say at once, however, that such formation of a Canon was not, and could not be, completed in pre-Christian times. For, on the one hand, Scriptures emerged when there were no prophets any longer. The writer of Scripture need not be a prophet, and many of the later Wisdom writings were doubtlessly written by authors who laid no claim to being prophets, whose message would be authentic in itself without needing the support of the Synagogue or of anybody else. On the other hand, the Synagogue as a religious institution, distinct from the prophets who appeared from time to time, could not itself attest with certainty this inspiration and canonicity. The formation of the Old Testament could, therefore, not have been concluded before the time of the Church. Knowledge of inspiration and formation of the Canon could begin because and inasmuch as there was prophecy which supported the writings. But no more than that. It is not surprising, therefore, that the Church accomplished the delimitation of the Old Testament Canon and did not take over a ready-made Canon from the Synagogue.[32]

[32] The rejection by Protestants of the deutero-canonical books as canonical and inspired because they were not acknowledged as such by the synagogue contradicts the fact that all the Old Testament books aim at Christ and the New Testament and are redemptive history only because of this reference, and can be recognized as such. If such reference to what is to come belongs to the essence of the Old Testament, we may ask whether this essence exists and is respected if the line between the canonical Old Testament history and Christ is historically broken and the past is thus torn from its future fulfilment in Christ. If this cannot be accepted, the question arises at the very "cessation" of the prophets whether we can still talk about divine effectiveness if that would conserve the history after the exile as sacred history aimed at Christ, which continues towards him through God and thus in the reality of history. When

But if the whole process of Scripture-making of the Old Testament, too, was only completed in the New Testament, it follows that the Scriptures of the Old Testament were ultimately produced by God inasmuch as they were to have (and preserve) their validity and function in the New Testament. The Old Testament is not only a *de facto* account of the prehistory of the Church and the truth, which was already recognized in this prehistory. It was thus designed, for its own essence could not otherwise be completed in the New Testament.

Now we may say according to our thesis that, inasmuch as God causes the Old Testament as the definitive image of the prehistory of the Church, he inspires the Scriptures and makes them his own as their author. In other words, because the Old Testament belongs *a priori* to the formation of the Church and not only of the Synagogue, as a part of her prehistory and as such remains actual for ever, it can claim the same validity as the New Testament.

Our thesis in regard to the inspiration of the New Testament is thus not abrogated by the fact of the inspiration of the Old Testament. On the contrary, it will be confirmed by showing that the longing for the New Testament belongs from the outset to the nature of the Old Testament and its writings. These books are subject to the same formative law as those of the New Testament.

the Church, as against Marcion and others, accepts the Old Testament as her own prehistory, as a part of her own as yet hidden life ("Church since Adam and Abel") this history cannot be something that has actually ceased long before; it is but a dead matter of the past or continues merely as man's history of religion.

III

CONCLUSIONS

ASSUMING that our thesis has been understood, we first intend finally to demonstrate that the essential elements traditionally postulated for divine authorship and inspiration are safeguarded in this conception; second, that we are now in a position to answer those questions which we posed in the first part of our investigation.

1. It follows from the basis of our thesis that God is the originator, the author of the Scriptures. By this we prove, at least, that God's authorship of the Scriptures, which is a truth of faith, is not in contradiction to our theological thesis.

God wills and produces the Scripture by a formal predefinition of a redemptive-historical and eschatological kind as a constitutive element of the foundation of the primitive Church,[33]

[33] The divine activity can be viewed from three special angles which altogether make up the particular nature of that divine activity which is here in question: a. It is an activity of formal predefinition analogous to the *gratia efficax;* b. This activity as such belongs to the visible history of the redemption. It moves in the dimension of pragmatic history and is expressed in it as predefining. Both aspects must be noted. A formal predefinition of a human act springing from the transcendental world, as it were, anonymously, would not constitute the result and work in a special degree really God's own. The predefining act of God may not only support the world as a whole and in it single happenings, as the divine causality supports everything in its totality and each thing indivi-

because and inasmuch as he wills and effects the primitive Church in exactly this manner. But to effect such a book is to be its author in an actual sense, because such an effect upon a book on account of our limited human vocabulary can even be described as authorship when we take into consideration that the divine authorship of the Bible is free from certain characteristics unavoidable in human authorship. The term authorship, therefore, used in regard to God and to man is an analogous concept only. God can thus be said to be the author of the Scriptures of the New Testament.

Regarding the major and minor of the syllogism we would add one remark. We have shown earlier that the current concept of inspiration, as it is explained by acknowledged theologians, may be taken as a very abstract, formal approach. How the elements of the concept of the inspiration are actually to be realized by God has been left open. We have said that, when God by himself only takes care (because he himself wills it in that way) that the human author under his influence should perceive correctly and effectively the judgement of what is to be written *(iudicium speculativum et practicum),* decides to write down what he has perceived, and undertakes his task,

dually, but it must operate from a particular point in space and time in preference to any other. It must operate in a redemptive-historical and miraculous manner. Only thus can it achieve its special reference to God, by virtue of which it can be said of God that he is "author". c. This predefining of a redemptive-historical kind has the same eschatological, final character also for the Scriptures which we claimed for the foundation of the Church, in contrast to pre-Christian redemptive history. This is not contradicted by the fact that there were inspired writings before Christ. For these were willed by God from the beginning as books of the eschatological community of redemption and are therefore all that we have inspiration and divine authorship, regardless of how the execution of this divine predefinition is thought to be realized. But we may add for the sake of any worried reader that the complete form of the divine realization of the Apostolic Church is, of course, "specified" according to the constituent (for instance, Scripture) in the total effect (Apostolic Church) which at any one time has to be realized. It would certainly not be irreconciliable with our basic idea to require a special kind of divine activity for the realization of a particular constituent (for instance, the composition of the Book of the Church) which are not needed for the realization of another constituent. If then, for some reason, more is thought to be needed for an intelligible concept of inspiration than what we hold to be necessary, this would not contradict our opinion that the divinely inspired authorship is an intrinsic constituent of the divine foundation of the Church. Moreover, this divine impulse, joined to God's will to establish the Church, must always reach down into the intellectual and volitive, spiritual sphere of man, for without such human activity, no Scripture

remains of real, historical, actual greatness in the Church from the Old Testament.

Through these three factors jointly the Scriptures gain an incomparable closeness in their original to God. This closeness is best expressed by saying that God is the originator and author of the Bible. We may recall that the authorship relation is of a fluid nature even in the human realm, and not as indivisible as is usually supposed in the theology of the inspiration. The human author can be more or less original; he may range from the creative thinker down to the copying "secretary" of his environment and the *Zeitgeist* who reflects the current clichés of speech and thought. From this angle there is no difficulty in characterizing God's authorship, claimed in our considerations, as one existing in an eminent sense.

could result. Thus, in this sense it is in any case also correct to hold that there is necessarily an intrinsic inspiration, even if we may leave it open whether or not this divine impulse, which spreads in the human spirit, must necessarily have its starting point within man. The origins of a book are necessarily dependent on its surrounding world. Without it there would not be the intellectual sphere, which is an essential condition for its intelligibility. Indeed, there would be more of a divine inspiration if we allow it to proceed from the redemptive-historical situation, in which the writing took place. The marvellous work of God, who is his own witness in history, is the realm in which the Scriptures emerge. Being Scriptures they originate in a predefined manner, and by originating in this realm, they are, *eo ipso,* Scriptures.

2. Finally, we would like to show why this conception is more likely, in our opinion, than others to solve the many questions with which we came into contact in the first part of our investigation. It will then be quite evident that it was not our object to juggle with logic by including a narrower concept (inspiring authorship) in a wider concept (active and predefining composition by the Church), because both concepts have certain formal points in common *(praedefinitio formalis),* and because we would use the trick of considering the former occurrence as part of the latter.

It is, we trust, easier to understand how God and man can both be authors of the same Scriptures. It becomes clear that both authorships are not aimed at the same effect. God does not, as it were, want *(intentione prima et per se)* to be a "writer"; he is one, because his will cannot otherwise be realized. God can achieve his first and last intention only by allowing man to be

writer and an author. In the familiar interpretation of inspiration, God's intention would be achieved even more perfectly
if man's function were but a secretary's. In our interpretation,
the opposite is the case. A man intends to write a book, and
he is to want to do this precisely according to God's ultimate
intention. God's will is a supernatural and historical community
of redemption, which finds its objective and self-realizing
ultimate end in the book. And, as he wills that community
effectively and absolutely, historically and eschatologically,
and in an historical process beginning anew in himself, God *eo
ipso* is, in a real sense, an author. Both authorships thus have a
terminative difference and, therefore, they can both be linked
with the same book, without either reducing the one or the
other to some merely verbal, meaningless concept, or misinter-
preting their coexistence as a joint undertaking. When we say
that God is the *auctor principalis,* but that men are the *auctores
secundarii* and *instrumentales,* we do not here regard inspiration
as only one case of a relationship which could occur elsewhere,
but we mean one unique relationship. In the writing of a
book, we can have no other *auctor principalis,* since any *auctor
instrumentalis* would in another case have secretarial functions
or conversely any *auctor principalis* could in reality impel or
cause the book to be written, but could not be its real author.

We shall also be able to understand more easily why the
history of God's authorship has no continuation. In the formal
concept of the inspiration there is no reason why this should
not happen. To rely on God's free and positive will is theology's
easiest way out and should be sparingly used. In the mere fact
that God's revelation is concluded, there is, indeed, no reason,
for new books could easily be written even about a completed

revelation and God could be their author. But if God appears as "author" only where the Church is yet "in growth" and has yet to be formed by divine, redemptive-historical and pre-defining action, then God's authorship ceases when the establishment of the Church is accomplished.[34]

The phenomenon of God's authorship, although the concept is used in a genuine and real, not merely metaphorical sense, is, therefore, something *sui generis* from the outset that includes an intrinsic quality which brings it about that God is to be originator and author in a sense which can apply only to God. There can be no other author apart from God who becomes an author by making man one. For God alone can impel man's freedom to act in such a way that this freedom and its product is formed by this impulse, and not limited or lessened by it. We could also say that the human authorship has, in a similar sense, *potentia oboedientialis* in regard to God, undiminished, indeed freed for highest achievements, in order to be taken up by God and by him alone, as for example free intellectual autonomy has the *potentia oboedientialis* in being embraced by a divine person to reach his own absolute perfection.

It cannot be claimed that all this also holds true in the traditional view of inspiration, as this conceives of inspiration

[34] The end of Revelation and the completion of the Church are obviously related. What is to be understood by "end" I have suggested in the article, "Zur Frage der Dogmenentwicklung" in *Schriften zur Theologie* (Einsiedeln, 1954), pp. 49–90, esp. 58 et seq. When we realize that God's revelation does not cease "because God will say no more, although he could well do so", but because the eschatological event of redemption, of which alone he speaks and to which also the Church belongs has occurred, we may see why the completion of the Church, and not the ending revelation, is here in question.

nalogously with the nature of efficient grace, just as we do. It s true that the traditional view explains occasionally why it is hat the authorship remains in human hands – the opposite of what is usually held, since it is commonly believed that God s the originator of the book *eo ipso* by impelling the writing ccording to the working of efficient grace.[35] But this view alone cannot explain how God, by means of such pre-defining notion, could become author. For this to happen, it is required hat his action, while respecting man's freedom, should really be on the level of redemptive history.[36] When we are asked to state

[35] If God, for example, by means of an efficient grace were to cause omebody by formal predefinition to make a table, God would not hereby become a carpenter, although the same could be said of this ausation which is said of inspiration: that he moves the intellect to con-ceive the idea and the plan, that he moves the will to decide the execution, hat he governs the execution itself in order that what is made should be exactly what was planned. We thus get the additional notion of God's ntervention in the earthly sphere, whence these movements are caused. Our criticism starts from the average understanding of efficient grace as it s commonly taught. We do not deny, though, that it would be possible o deepen this concept of efficient grace so that it would include also the redemptive-historical factor: grace as grace which is always the grace of the incarnate Word: grace which always includes reference to faith, which derives from its acceptance in history; grace which is always grace of the Church going out from her – and tending towards her. If this deepened concept of grace were to be related to with efficient grace *qua* efficient, if morever, this concept of efficacious grace were used as model for the freely given grace of inspiration and the explanation of its nature, we might ask where is the redemptive-historical factor in inspiration? And on the strength of the traditional parallel between efficiacous grace and inspiration, which is a customary point of departure, one might also arrive at our proposed theory.

[36] However, not all occurrences coming from God are themselves also historical events. The movement of the sun through divine con-currance does not signify, for instance, an historical action on God's part

how and where this is the case, we might retort by asking th
traditionalists where it is that they discover this level of inspira
tion, and whether this is of such a kind that human authorshi
would be admitted, not just verbally, but also in reality, indee
calling for it.

We are also in a position to give a more detailed answer t
the question whether or not inspiration could be an unconsciou
process. When we take the abstract, formalized concept o
inspiration simply for the thing itself, thus excluding its whol
meaning, an affirmative answer is necessary. Inspiration in tha
case is unconscious. But if the meaning of the concept is included
as we sought to do, the answer is more likely to be negative
The life of the Church-to-be who finds herself in the Scripture
is, on the one hand, conscious (a consciousness, indeed, with
supernatural and miraculous components) and, on the othe
hand, it reaches into inspiration and its consciousness, at least
when and inasmuch as the human author knows himself in hi
writing to be carried by that living process of the Church
believing in the Holy Spirit. But again, this consciousness nee
not directly effect our formalized concept of inspiration and o
the authorship of God. An author of a part of the New Testa-

although the movement of the sun occurs in space and time and is, therefore, historical. In miracles and in formal self-revelations God himself acts
historically. Through his action he intervenes in the chain of events, no
supporting the chain only as a whole. However, only God can do thi
when this event is also manifested *quoad nos,* when it has the character of a
sign, happening by announcing itself and announcing itself by happening
Miracles which would not be known absolutely would really be open to
the rationalists' charge that God tinkers about with his world and it
course. Canonicity and inspiration are indeed more closely linked than
is usually admitted.

ment, in our view, need not necessarily know of his own inspiration. There is no need for him to say that in regard to this very part, possibly an unimportant section, he is under God's special influence. And yet he could have been conscious of a special "inspiration" by God (of an intellectual and voluntary nature) concomitantly inasmuch as he knew while writing that its real core was given through God's self-revelation in Christ. This occurred in the writer's own generation, and was confirmed through that holy community, to which he belongs, which was then becoming the model for all future teaching and activity. Whether or not this consciousness formally (though implicitly) includes the whole of inspiration, need not be discussed here. We repeat that inspiration need not at all be a conscious process. In our theory, however, the conscious elements are part of the essential meaning of inspiration, and not only its remote conditions. Inspiration is, thus, a conscious process. Unconscious in it would be at most the fact that the book has been caused by God as a permanent document of the self-knowledge achieved by the Church in her future. Where this element has been conscious in some form, for instance, in the gospels, we could say in view of our theory that inspiration had been – although under aspects less usual today - wholly conscious.

We may now also better understand how the Church recognizes the inspiredness of the Bible. It is correct to maintain that ultimately the inspiredness of a writing can be known only through revelation; all other paths of knowledge are of no avail in this question. But the question is only how this revelation is to be conceived, so that its course and first proclamation can be conceived with historical plausibility. It is held that the apostles must have signified which books were inspired. It is without doubt true that the actual occurrence of this revelation must be concluded "with the death of the last apostle", as it is somewhat oddly expressed. But how are we to imagine this "proclamation" by a particular apostle so that this action should be historically probable?[37] Beyond the *a priori* postulate that something like that must have occurred there is no further information.[38] But is this postulated process likely to have occurred in view of the hesitation and fluctuations in the history of the Canon? These historical difficulties are usually explained

[37] A. Bea, op. cit., no. 114, says simply: "quomodo et cui illi prima revelatio facta sit, plerumque ignoramus." Certainly the living and authentic voice of the Church guarantees, as Bea emphasizes, that this revelation has occurred. And that may suffice for the ordinary faithful. But, when the teaching authority contains no new revelation, but only continues to affirm, indeed infallibly, what it has heard, the theologian cannot simply be satisfied with the testimony of the teaching authority, but has to try to explain whence the authority now teaching has obtained its teaching. He has to show how this doctrine was first expressed by an apostle, or how it is contained in some other truth. But how are we to do this if Bea is right, and what he says is all that can be said? For it is not likely that at the time when the faith-consciousness of the Church and her teaching authority attained clarity regarding the canonicity of a scripture one would still have known, *quomodo et cui illa prima revelatio* (on the inspiredness of that book) *facta sit*.

[38] It is not contested that the bulk of the New Testament writings was transmitted by the Apostolic Church from the earliest times as canonical. But this does not lessen the problem in regard to many other New Testament writings. And we may ask whether the same problem of recognizing the canonicity did not also apply to the bulk of the New Testament writings and in their case was only solved earlier. It was solved at a time which we can no longer penetrate – without having to assume for each writing an explicit and formal tradition back to an explicit statement by an apostle, which supposition would lack all historical probability.

by assuming that the tradition about the inspiredness of particular books first was handed down only in individual churches, that it took some time until the news spread to the whole Church and was universally accepted. But what about those traditional "opinions" in other churches, in which certain writings were accepted as canonical and inspired which actually were not (Epistle of Barnabas, The Pastor of Hermas, etc.)? How were the two traditions differentiated? What was the rule in making the distinction? It would not seem to be historically convincing that in the one case, it was possible for the tradition to be traced back to an explicit statement from an apostle, where as, in the other case, this test was shown to be impossible. How are we then to imagine the knowledge, which developed in time, of the inspiredness and canonicity of individual writings?

If our proposed thesis is right, we have a way out of this deadlock. We have but to distinguish between the basic revelation as such (as a process) about the inspiration of a book on the one hand, and the written grasp and discussion of this revelation on the other hand. The former must have been completed on the death of the last apostle, but not the latter. Both obviously cannot, however, have a different timing when, as it is always presupposed, the revelation of the inspiredness of a writing has to be expressed in some explicit statement about it. But this presupposition has to be contested. Our theory shows that this is not necessary at all. This revelation is simply given by the fact that the relevant writing emerges as a genuine self-expression[39] of the primitive Church. Her inspiredness is thereby

[39] Self-expression naturally does not mean that in each (even small and occasional) Scripture the whole essence of the faith of the Church is expressed, but only that it mirrors truly (actively and passively) the

65

sufficiently revealed, unless we were to assume that something could be revealed only by a direct statement and not also by some immediately perceptible fact which would, however imply a much too narrow, false and conceptual idea of the possibilities of revelation.[40] The fact presenting itself, given by God's supernatural, redemptive-historical operation, can be perceived and also expressed even in post-apostolic times, without the occurrence of any new revelation. This is not controverted when we have to assume that only the Church herself has that gift of absolutely sure judgement, which is necessary in order to find out whether some particular writing from apostolic times is not an intrinsic homogeneous piece of the self-constitution of the Church. It is wrong to think that, for the accurate understanding of what has been revealed from the factors proposed in the history of the development of dogma, we must have a link with the forms of rational-conceptual deduction. The Church, filled with the Holy Spirit, recognizes something as connatural amongst the writings which accord with her nature. If, at the same time, it is also "apostolic", that is, a piece of the self-accomplishment of the Apostolic Church

primitive Church. This relationship between the Scripture and the faith which obtains an essential expression in it, is not to be thought of as if the various writings of the New Testament, as material-quantitative parts, would add up to the basic document of faith, just as the parts of a catechism do, of which each part deals with something else, and would make up the whole catechism. Each part reflects the whole of the essence of the faith of the primitive Church, without being only a material part of the adequate expression of this essence. Therefore, in our theory, the view is not disputed that many books in the New Testament, judged from the direct vision of individual human authors, are "occasional" writings.

[40] Cf. K. Rahner, *Schriften zur Theologie,* i (Einsiedeln, 1954), pp. 49–90.

as such, and recognized as such, it is then, according to the assumptions of our theory, inspired *eo ipso* without any need (even if actually the reflex response only happens much later) to refer to a revelation in that sense, or to postulate that the recognition has to be contemporaneous with the revelation. Thus, we have a real historical space for the history of the Canon. If we suppose the conscious knowledge of canonicity to be the result of an explicit and direct testimony by an apostle, as is usually done, then we cannot really understand how it could take so long, until the canonicity of many writings was finally explained. In such a case one would even be forced – *sit venia verbo* – to use the excuse that the whole matter was clear at one time, then the confusion arose in some way in order, finally, in a third phase, for the Church to arrive at definite and explicit clarity. But this seems to be an excuse, because, historically, we do not know of a period of clarity in regard to the inspiration of certain writings (we mean an inspiredness as such and not only something very near to it). Such a statement is thus no more than an *a priori* postulate from premises which are not safe and which also involve historical improbability. If we distinguish, however, between the beginning of revelation of the inspiredness of a writing, though not in an explicit statement about it, but through the real growth of this book as a self-expression of the primitive Church on the one hand, and the rational acknowledgement of this writing as belonging to the self-constitution of the primitive Church on the other, seeing in the latter knowledge of inspiration and of the canonicity of the Bible, it is clear that this latter process needs time, has necessarily a history of its own, though the revelation of inspiration itself need not on that account require the same

67

duration. The history of the Canon would then be freed from those bewildering aspects with which the current view of inspiration has to grapple.

We might ask ourselves whether the correct and indispensible teaching, that an inspired work must have originated before the death of the last apostle (cf. Pesch, *De inspiratione,* no. 602), is not frequently interpreted (without any need) somewhat too materially. If the "death of the last apostle" signifies the first generation of the Church, the period of her coming into being, as distinct from her continuation as a body constituted for all time, the statement will be immediately understandable. Less obvious, however, is the supposition that this period of the formative Church ended necessarily on the day in the calendar when the last apostle died. Is such a deduction from the right meaning of the statement in question really justified? Have we to assume it as absolutely certain before investigating, say, the literary characteristics of the Epistle to the Hebrews, or of the Second Epistle of St. Peter, or even perhaps of one of the pastoral letters, that these documents could not have originated after that day and need not only belong to the first generation? What point could there be to our study of the inspiredness of later writings not written by an apostle if, quite somewhere else, an apostle, perhaps St. John, was still alive, whose knowledge of these writings and explicit transmission of their inspiredness is very improbable?

For even if we could assume his knowledge, we might ask whence he knew about their inspiredness. As Christians, we are bound to hold that the men of the early Church had a certain knowledge, through miracles, etc., of the divine authorship and of the events of the redemption, of which they have been objects and witnesses. But could we as easily assume that a particular apostle would, regarding a certain smaller writing, receive a special revelation about the divine authorship? While it is not impossible to accept such an awkward assumption, is it really necessary? Or could we explain this knowledge on the lines on which we have suggested? But if our explanation is right or, at least, acceptable, ought this recognition of the inspiredness necessarily refer to an apostle, or could it not occur elsewhere also, through the Church? In which latter case, there would seem to be no obstacle to the possibility that this knowledge might relate to a writing which belonged to the first generation, but need not have been written before the death of the last apostle. Obviously, the concept of the first generation is somewhat vague, but this does not seem to be unacceptable. For if, indeed, there might have been a decade or so in which it would have difficult to state with absolute certainty whether or not the Apostolic Church was "past", the time would have certainly been at hand when it could be said that it was over. We may use the comparison of the approach of death: the fact that there are moments in which it is, as yet, impossible to say that it has arrived, cannot preclude that there are moments in which it has certainly occurred. The necessity for safe criteria for the beginning of a process – death, the end of the Apostolic Church, etc. – need not imply the existence of such criteria, which could decide the problem at every moment. Twenty years, for example, after the death of the last apostle (about the turn of the first century A.D.) at a time when it was already possible to look back to an earlier and "different" age, it could certainly be stated that the time of the Apostolic Church was past.

69

If the emergence of the Scriptures as books of the Apostolic Church is the very reason why they have God as author, the relationship of inspired writings and teaching authority also becomes clearer. We comprehend that these two factors do not cancel each other out, but need each other. The Church as a factor of the end of time, as God's ultimate community of redemption, cannot be followed by any other event in time and in the world. She awaits but the glory of God directly revealed. She is triumphant, infallible. For she is this Church as bearer and believer of this final revelation of God, which is revealed as his final triumphant mercy. Otherwise a new revelation of God would have to follow her, or the phase of grace could be followed already in this world by a period of the condemning wrath of God. Where the Church takes possession of her faith in such an absolutely binding manner by witnessing (teaching) and by listening (believing), the gates of Hell cannot prevail against her. In the case of her hierarchical structure, infallibility in the first place attaches to the faithful witnesses and messengers of the Lord, the twelve apostles. Their infallibility naturally continues for the duration of time and of her existence. Nevertheless it is not only something which, like a formal potency, is always newly given to the Church, so that the infallibility of the later time (though similar to that of the earlier) would still be, in every respect, independent of it. The potency of the later period is the potency of infallible custody of the earlier, the potency of persisting in the teaching of the apostles. The link with this teaching must not be understood only as a link with the meaning of this teaching. That is also included, but not only that. There is also the link with the act of this teaching and its infallibility. Any appeal or reference to the earlier teaching would be meaningless, unless at the same time this earlier doctrine is actually believed and announced as infallible. The act of an unerring teaching by means of which the Church at a particular time has made herself the final community of redemptive truth, and at that same time has become Church, is an act performed in virtue of the earlier infallibility, and its formal continuation. It is not only of the same kind as the earlier act, as two realizations of the same species would be, but the further expression in time of what is, formally, the same act. This obviously does not imply the same physical bearer or physical identity. But the first act of the Church was at least accomplished through the composition of the Scriptures. For the teaching of the early Church has not only found factual expression also in the Scriptures; the Scriptures are the canonical exposition of this teaching of the early Church. They emerge as the act of the early Church teaching infallibly. This obviously implies that the particular author of a particular part of the Bible – which in its literary form does not include this intention – wrote it as one belonging to the self-revealing Church at least in as much as this was intended and effected by God from the beginning. To recognize this in the case of a particular document of the early Church would, of course, require only that the Church should still have in her possession this writing even after the end of the early Church and recognize it as her genuine expression. However, if in the early, growing Church the act of this teaching, in which she establishes herself also for later times as the norm and to which every later act will necessarily refer back, is an act of composition of the Scripture, then it is obvious that the act of the later infallible teaching Church will appear essentially also as an act of reference to the Scripture.

There is no clash between two infallibilities. First, they are not established independently from each other. They are not designed later to find arrangements for mutual coexistence without cancelling each other out. They have reference to each other from the beginning like two instances of the same process. The problem of possible contradiction *a priori* is eliminated. In order to understand the nature of the one, the other has to be understood. Infallibility of the teaching authority of the later Church is, by definition, the inerrant interpretation of the Scripture, because it includes by definition the link with the teaching of the early Church, which necessarily teaches the later Church and has expressed her teaching in the Scripture.

If we may advance our concept of the sufficiency of Scriptures against the Two Sources Theory, we can even go a step further and say that the infallible teaching authority of the early Church in her function for the future is the capacity for creating the Scriptures. The infallible teaching office of the Church *after* the early Church is the authoritative interpretation of the Bible. Naturally, these statements would be badly misunderstood if taken to mean that in practice they could be used by individual Christians as a criterion whether the Church was right or wrong in her teaching. Of course, when the Church teaches according to the norms of her office (whereby the competence of competent authorities that entails the right handling of these norms cannot be checked by individuals), we have thereby the guarantee that the Bible has been interpreted correctly. The Church possesses the Scripture, not only as a book, approaching it as it were from the outside like an unbelieving historian or exegete, in order to investigate what she can use out of it in regard to this or that question. The Church possesses the Scripture as something written and always read and accomplished in her own life. The reference to this earlier reading of the Bible is also part of the "oral tradition", which is there without our having to assume for it the Two Sources Theory. This theory has actually been adopted because it is widely thought that the facts of the development of dogma, as it really occurred, could not be explained by the principle of material sufficiency of the Scripture, and by the total, material dependence of the later Church on the Scriptures. But then we get a book composed by God himself and still not sufficient, not even in regard to the function of this book, namely the communication of that which God has revealed.

In order to understand the sufficiency of the Bible we might consider: 1. The sufficiency of the Scripture (even by rejecting the Two Sources Theory) does not signify the elimination of "oral tradition". There can be no such elimination. The oral tradition is an essential and necessary postulate of the living and binding teaching authority of the Church, and is thus "tradition". It is well known that difficulties are still encountered in Catholic theology distinguishing between the teaching office, or between "active tradition" and authoritative pronouncements on the one hand, and what is handed down by this tradition and was taught authoritatively in earlier times on the other. Nor is the oral tradition excluded, inasmuch as the Scriptures in the Church are not only something written, but also read and understood independently from the understanding of the faith in the early Church which is prior to the Scripture. The earlier tradition of the Scripture interpretation is, for the later Church, both norm and part of the oral tradition.

2. Naturally, the sufficiency of the Scriptures does not mean

that the late unfolding of their meaning, which is the development of dogma, could be rejected by the individual Christian with the argument that the Bible sufficed for him. Precisely because the Scriptures are an objectivization of the "beginnings" of the faith in the early Church and carry within themselves the essential characteristics of historical development, the sufficiency of the Bible is, as it were, a living protest against its mummification and reduction to the level of a dead letter. The Church derives her life from her own beginning, thus from her Scriptures, and has no other beginning beside and beyond it. It is, however, of the essence of this beginning, that it is not also the end. It is not only not the end of theology, but also it is not the end (of the unfolding) of the faith and of the authoritative teaching of the Church.

3. To reject the sufficiency of the Bible, would not, indeed, make it easier to explain the facts of the development of dogma. We might test this statement by asking which of those dogmas of the Church that were defined in later times can be traced back more easily to their origin from apostolic preaching of the original revelation of God in Christ when we look for this origin in the oral tradition and not in the Scriptures? There will be no such examples. In the case of a dogma, for which it is hard to find a scriptural basis, it can, of course, always be said that it was contained, and must be contained, in the oral tradition even if this could not be proved. But the same postulate (in our presupposition) can be asserted even more easily in regard to the Scriptures. The later dogma must be contained in it, even if it is not now possible to see clearly in the researches of individual theologians how it is contained therein. Moreover, in such a case, the appeal to the oral tradition would be useful only if it

could be shown historically that, in fact, there was such an oral tradition of a particular dogma beside the Scriptures. Naturally, as a Catholic, I know that when the Church defines something as revealed by God, then it must have been contained, explicitly or implicitly, in the original apostolic teaching. However, once this conclusion has been reached, it is still the task of theology to consider where and how all this can be demonstrated historically. For, conscious as the Church has to be, and is already when defining the dogma, of the link between it and the oral or written early tradition, such a consciousness need not necessarily have that degree of explicitness to make superfluous any further theological research in this respect. But it will be impossible to quote examples in which this reference to early tradition would succeed better by substituting the oral tradition for the Scripture. In other words, which statement of a modern dogma could be demonstrated as having been taught by the apostles, handed down as such, the process of tradition being also historically traceable, without the dogma being also contained explicitly or implicity in the Scripture? Thus the assumption of a Two Sources Theory by no means facilitates the explanation of the development of dogmas.

4. The difficulties encountered in the history of dogmas through the material sufficiency of the Scriptures chiefly stem from a too narrow concept of the process of interpretation. If only that is regarded as legitimate interpretation of something already implicitly contained in the Scripture, which by a purely private, formal-logical analysis could be known by any individual alone, this interpretation would not be sufficient to explain the factual development of dogmas from the Scriptures. But neither would it be sufficient to explain it from the oral tradition. Nor

75

would it serve for cases such as the Nicene, Ephesian, Chalcedonian dogmas which the whole of Christendom accept as binding, thereby appealing to the Scripture without considering any further material source of the faith. Nor would it serve unless the fact of habit is taken for a proof in such cases where the Church declares explicitly, that this dogma is in the Scriptures (Original Sin: Rom. 5; Sacrament of Penance; John 20, etc.). However, if we presuppose a less narrow concept of interpretation (which it is not our task to explain here), there will be no greater difficulty in tracing a modern dogma back to the Scriptures than by wanting not only to postulate but also to demonstrate this reference back to an unwritten oral primitive tradition.

On the basis of our thesis we might also arrive at a less embarrassed attitude towards the fact in the history of religion, that non-Christian religions of a high cultural level also have their holy books. It does not seem that our theological writings on inspiration have paid sufficient, serious and unprejudiced attention to this fact. There is no reason to be afraid of the comparisons. A community will establish itself as historically founded and enduring into the future, almost necessarily through books. It could even be suggested that this is the origin of these writings rather than the need for private communications. Such a book is thus an analogy or homology, which must be expected *a priori* in those religions which presuppose a certain cultural level and conceive themselves as a historical revealed religion. If we add to this that Christianity is a real act of the living God in history in a unique sense, then all the rest follows by itself, and the non-Christian analogies to the Holy Scriptures of Christianity need be suspected no longer. The idea of God as an author of books will lose the suggestion of naive anthropomorphism.

On the basis of our main thesis, it would also be easier to understand why the literary genera of the Scriptures do not reflect *eo ipso,* necessarily and absolutely, on God. God, for example, did not write a letter to Philemon, although he is the author of the epistle. Why not? Because he is author by willing absolutely and effectively that the Church as a community of love should manifest for all ages "canonically" her nature, her faith and her love, even in such a letter. Because God wills this letter in this way, which is not the way of human action, although precisely on this account it must aim at the action of man, the literary form will not affect God's authorship in a specific manner.

From our angle, it might also be more easily explained why the most varied literary forms are possible in the inspired writings. For if it is once realized that the *genus litterarium* is not simply that of the divine author, the question, which literary forms are suitable for God, is not difficult to face. This again has its bearings on the inerrancy of the Bible. The inerrant meaning of particular writings and sections has to be determined essentially from the literary forms of the writing. If it emerges that this literary form is not God's own work, then it can be expected that, on this basis also, the dogmatic teaching on the inerrancy of the Scripture can be applied to the particular cases. It still holds true that whatever the human writer wishes to say as true is true and is his opinion, and he expects us to accept that as true – that too is what God said and, therefore, free from error. Regarding the literary form, however, for which the man alone is responsible and which is not God's, it will be necessary in

77

many cases to limit closely and carefully what the writer really wanted to say.

The relationship between inspiration and canonicity also could be made clearer, and the close link between both brought home to us. In that respect, a distinction could be introduced between canonicity proper, a concept relating to the post-apostolic Church, (inspiredness rationally known and taught through the Church) and being a constituent part of the Church, a concept relating to the Apostolic Church that may not be identified simply with canonicity. This appertaining to the Apostolic Church belongs to the concept of inspiration, but its kinship with canonicity facilitates the understanding of the material and noetic link between inspiration and canonicity.

The circle of personalities of the inspired authors, too, will become more familiar. Among the authors of writings which share in the establishing of the Church are the apostles, but others also, inasmuch as their work at that time was representative of the Church, a means of her self-possession. By this we understand why, in the New Testament, the secondary, occasional writings (private epistles), inasmuch as they are inspired, are always by apostles (Philemon; Rom. 16:1–23; 2 and 3 John). Other authors (Mark, Luke) may "claim" by more representative works only to be models for the Church, while the apostles (obviously not in cases of profane writings) may always claim to be the fundaments of the Church. Such a view naturally presupposes that a letter from an apostle which was lost, must have been inspired, even though not canonical. There is no basic difficulty in such an assumption,[41] at least not according to our view. Whether it is meaningful that God should allow a letter

[41] Cf. A. Bea, op. cit., no. 125.

to be lost which was willed by him *prima intentione* and *per se* as his writing may be a different question. That small parts of a whole work which was intended by God to be, as a whole, the self-expression of the Church, should be lost, does not seem to be surprising. It is as little surprising as the fact that even individual sentences of inspired writings have been lost, which cannot be doubted.

Perhaps our thesis might also stimulate a new interest in some basic principles concerning the interpretation of the Bible.[42] If the author writes *a priori* as a member of the Church, then interpretation, if it is to be correct and adequate, has to observe two points, that he writes as a *member* of the Church, and that he writes as a member of the *Church*. Because he is only an individual member of the Church, and not the mere spokesman of an abstract Church, which always should have to speak as a whole, he has his own gift, which is not simply the whole, of all the gracious gifts of the Church, all her insight, all her faith, in all its possible developments.

We need to have a biblical exegesis which studies the mere particularized, autonomous, individual, theological physiognomy of an individual scripture and practises biblical theology in a stricter sense (in contrast to the use of the Scripture in dogmatics), allowing the particular writing to express itself in its theological individuality for itself and reducing everything *a priori* to a total theology. On the other hand, every author as a member of the *Church,* was open towards the whole of the Church, believed and taught within the Church and was

---

[42] Cf., e.g. Bea, "Bulla ineffabilis Deus et Hermeneutica Biblica" in *Virgo Immaculata. Acta Congressus Mariologici-Mariani Romae anno MCMLIV celebrati III* (Rome, 1955), pp. 1–17.

in his own theology always integrated, even there where he himself could not have surveyed it explicitly, into the universal theology of the one and whole Church of his own times. Otherwise, such a writing could not be regarded as "canonical" – which means, part of the conscious faith and the essential attitude of the Church – as acknowledged by the Church. It means in no way an adulteration or degrading of the individual author, or of his theology, but something that was experienced, in fact, by all the authors, that their own theology is spiritually embedded, included in the greater whole of the Church. If, therefore, the interpretation of a particular writing proceeds from the whole Scripture and from the Church and takes the rules and the norms from there, such a method could not be suspected *a priori* as being wrong. It follows from the very nature of the subject, provided that it remains clear where it differs from the other valid method which was described at the beginning of our thesis.

(1)